100 LITERACY FRAMEWORK LESSONS

TERMS AND CONDITIONS

IMPORTANT - PERMITTED USE AND WARNINGS - READ CAREFULLY BEFORE USING

YEAR 5

Scottish Primary 6

Minimum specification:
- PC and Mac with a CD-ROM drive and 512 Mb RAM (recommended)
- Windows 98SE or above/Mac OSX.1 or above
- Recommended minimum processor speed: 1 GHz

For all technical support queries, please phone
Scholastic Customer Services on 0845 603 9091

Isabel Macdonald

CREDITS

Author
Isabel Macdonald

Commissioning Editor
Fiona Tomlinson

Development Editor
Simret Brar

Project Editor
Rachel Mackinnon

Assistant Editor
Kate Stenner

Series Designers
Anna Oliwa &
Joy Monkhouse

Designer
Sonia Bagley, Yen Fu &
Micky Pledge

Book Designer
Q2A Media

Illustrations
Dusan Pavlic / Beehive
Illustration

CD-ROM Development
CD-ROM developed in
association with Vivid
Interactive

ACKNOWLEDGEMENTS

The publishers gratefully acknowledge permission to reproduce the following copyright material: **Jane Bower** for the use of a recipe for 'Raspberry buns' by Jane Bower from *Junior Education Topics* February 2006 © 2006, Jane Bower (2006, Scholastic Ltd). **Pie Corbett** for the use of 'Wings' by Pie Corbett from *The Works: Key Stage 2* © 2006, Pie Corbett (2006, Macmillan Children's Books). **Beverly Curl** for the reuse of illustrations from 'Raspberry Buns' which appeared in *Junior Education Topics* February 2006 issue © 2006, Beverly Curl (2006, Scholastic Ltd). **Eddison Pearson** for the use of 'Whose dem boots' by Valerie Bloom from *The world is sweet* by Valerie Bloom © 2000, Valerie Bloom (2000, Bloomsbury). **Egmont UK** for the use of illustrations from *Kensuke's Kingdom* by Michael Morpurgo. Illustrations © 1999, Michael Foreman (1999, Egmont UK Ltd). **Her Majesty's Stationery Office** the use of extracts from *The Primary National Strategy* © Crown copyright, reproduced under the terms of The PSI Licence. **David Higham Associates** for the use of an illustration from *The Lottie Project* by Jacqueline Wilson. Illustration © 1997, Nick Sharratt (1997, Doubleday); an extract from *Arthur, High King of Britain* by Michael Morpurgo © 1994, Michael Morpurgo (1994, Pavilion Books Ltd); extracts from *The Ghost of Thomas Kempe* by Penelope Lively © 1973, Penelope Lively (1973, Heinemann Young Books) and extracts from *Kensuke's Kingdom* by Michael Morpurgo © 1999, Michael Morpurgo (1999, Egmont UK Ltd). **Hodder and Stoughton Ltd** for the use of an extract and an illustration from *Earth watch: Water for all* produced for Franklin Watts by Bender Richardson White ©2000, Franklin Watts (2000, Franklin Watts) and for the use of extracts from 'Bre-Nancy and the 13 plantains' by Petronella Breinburg from *Multi-cultural stories: stories from the Caribbean* by Petronella Breinberg © 1999, Wayland Publishers Ltd (1999, Wayland Publishers Ltd). **Jack Ousbey** for the use of 'Gran can you rap?' by Jack Ousbey from *All in the family* edited by John Foster © 1993, Jack Ousbey (1993, Oxford University Press). **Oxford University Press** for the use of an extract from 'Spider's web' from *Tales from Africa* retold by Kathleen Arnott © 1962, Kathleen Arnott (1962; 2000, Oxford University Press) and 'Come to Greece' from *The Greeks: Teacher's Notes* by Isabel Macdonald © 2003, Isabel Macdonald (2003, Oxford University Press). **Campbell Perry** for the use of 'The wrong bag' playscript by Campbell Perry from *50 Literacy hours for less able learners: Ages 7 to 9* by Julie Coyne © 2005, Campbell Perry (2005, Scholastic Ltd) and for the use of 'Amul and the Drum' and 'Fairground' both by Campbell Perry from *All new 100 literacy hours: Year 5* by Chris Webster © 2005, Campbell Perry (2005, Scholastic Ltd, and for the use of 'Plane crazy', 'The sun', 'The sea woman', 'Jason and the golden fleece', 'Pandora's box' and 'Face' all by Campbell Perry © 2007, Campbell Perry (2007, previously unpublished). **Jillian Powell** for the use of text from *Read and Respond: Kensuke's Kingdom* by Jillian Powell © 2007, Jillian Powell (2007, Scholastic Ltd). **The Random House Group** for the use of extracts from *The Lottie Project* by Jacqueline Wilson © 1997, Jacqueline Wilson (1997, Doubleday). **Scholastic Children's Books** for the use of a webpage from 'The Zone' on www.scholastic.co.uk © 2007, Scholastic Ltd (2007, Scholastic Ltd). **Jane Serraillier Grossfeld** for the use of 'The Visitor' by Ian Serraillier from *A Second Poetry Book* compiled by John Foster © 1980, The Estate of Ian Serraillier (1980, Oxford University Press). **Celia Warren** for the use of 'Cold morning' by Celia Warren from *All new 100 literacy hours: Year 5* by Chris Webster © 2005, Celia Warren (2005, Scholastic Ltd). **Chris Webster** for the use of 'Stop animal testing' from *All new 100 literacy hours: Year 5* by Chris Webster © 2005, Chris Webster (2005, Scholastic Ltd). **Kit Wright** for the use of 'The frozen man' by Kit Wright from *Rabbitting on* by Kit Wright © 1978, Kit Wright (1978 Young, Lions) and 'All of us' by Kit Wright from *The Works Key Stage 2* chosen by Pie Corbett © 2006, Kit Wright (2006, Macmillan Children's Books).

Every effort has been made to trace copyright holders for the works reproduced in this book, and the publishers apologise for any inadvertent omissions.

Text © 2007, Isabel Macdonald
© 2007, Scholastic Ltd

Designed using Adobe InDesign

Published by Scholastic Ltd
Villiers House
Clarendon Avenue
Leamington Spa
Warwickshire CV32 5PR

Visit our website at
www.scholastic.co.uk

Printed by Bell and Bain Ltd
3456789 7890123456

British Library Cataloguing-in-Publication Data
A catalogue record for this book is available from the British Library.
ISBN 978-0439-94525-7

CONTENTS

INTRODUCTION
100 Literacy Framework Lessons: Year 5

About the series

The *100 Literacy Framework Lessons* series is a response to the Primary National Strategy's revised Literacy Framework and contains **all new** material. The lessons mirror the structure and learning objectives of the Exemplification Units of the Framework. The CD-ROM provides appropriate and exciting texts and also contains a variety of other resources from videos and images to audio and weblinks, which will help to guide you in implementing the Framework's emphasis on ICT texts. The books and CD-ROMs will be an invaluable resource to help you understand and implement the revised Framework.

The key points of the revised framework are:
- The development of early reading and phonics;
- Coherent and progressive teaching of word-level and sentence-level embedded into learning or taught discretely;
- Following and building upon the teaching sequence from reading to writing and developing comprehension;
- Flexible lessons providing a challenging pace;
- Integration of speaking and listening skills;
- Planning for inclusion;
- Broadening and strengthening pedagogy.

Early reading and phonics

The authors of the *100 Literacy Framework Lessons* have endeavoured to incorporate all of the above with one exception, the teaching of phonics. The Government is advising that phonics is taught using a systematic, discrete and time-limited programme. However, where possible we have made links to phonic focuses that you might want to identify when teaching the lesson.

It is important to note that the renewed Framework is advocating a change from the Searchlight model of teaching early reading to the 'simple view of reading', *"The knowledge and skills within the four Searchlight strategies are subsumed within the two dimensions of word recognition and language comprehension of the 'two simple views of reading'. For beginner readers, priority should be given to securing word recognition, knowledge and skills"* (from the PNS Core Papers document). Phonic work will be time limited and as children develop their early reading skills they will then move from learning to read to learning to learn.

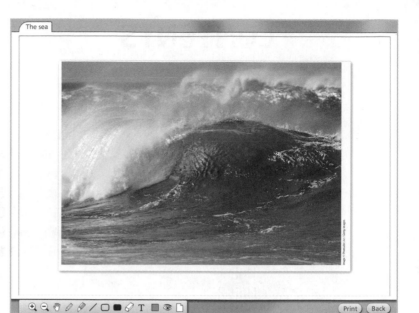

Using the book

The book is divided into three parts, called Blocks: Narrative Block, Non-fiction Block and Poetry Block. This reflects the structure of the renewed Framework planning. The Blocks are divided into Units, each Unit covers a different text-type within the Block, for example in the Narrative Block there might be one Unit which covers 'myths and legends' and another that covers 'plays'. Units are taught on a specified amount of weeks and are split into Phases. Phases vary in length and are essentially a way to focus on a specific part of teaching relating to the Unit. Phases are then divided into days, or lessons, which then contain the teaching activities. Unlike the *100 All New Literacy Hours,* this book has not been divided into terms because one of the main points of the Framework is flexibility and this structure will let teachers adapt to their particular children's needs.

Block [genre] ➤ Units [text-type] ➤ Phases [section of Unit] ➤ Days/Lessons [Individual lessons]

Units

Each Unit covers a different text-type, or genre and because of this each Unit has its own introduction containing the following:
Objectives: All objectives for the Unit are listed under their strand names.
Progression: Statements about the progression that the children should make within the Unit's focus, for example narrative text-type.
Aspects of learning: Key aspects of learning that the Unit covers.
Prior learning: Key elements that the children need to be able to do before they commence the lessons.
Cross-curricular opportunities: Integrating other areas of the curriculum into the literacy lessons.
Resources: Everything required for the lesson that teachers may not have readily available.
Teaching sequence: This is an overview chart of the Unit. It shows the number of Phases, children's objectives, a summary of activities and the learning outcomes.

Unit lesson plans

The lesson plans all follow the same format. There are three columns and each contains different information.
Key features: The key features column provides an at-a-glance view of the key aspects of learning covered in the lesson.
Stages: The stages column provides the main lesson plans.
Additional opportunities: This column provides additional opportunities for the lesson. This is where there will be links made to phonics, high frequency words, support or extension activities and any other relevant learning opportunities.

End of Phase

At the end of each Phase there are three boxes containing Guided reading or writing ideas, Assessment ideas and Further work.

Guided: The guided box contains ideas for guided reading or writing. These have been included separately as there seems to be a trend to do this work outside of the literacy hour lesson. These ideas can either be integrated into a lesson or taught at a separate time.

Assessment: There are two types of assessment.

End of Phase assessments: These are mainly observations of the children or simple tasks to see whether they have understood what has been taught in the Phase. Teachers are referred back to the learning outcomes in the teaching sequence in the Unit introduction.

End of Unit assessments: These are activities which range from interactive activities, to working from a stimulus image, to completing a photocopiable sheet. They can be found on the CD-ROM accompanying this series.

Further work: Further work provides opportunities for the teacher to extend or support the children following the assessment activity.

Photocopiable pages

At the end of each Unit are the photocopiable pages; these can also be found on the CD-ROM.

Using the CD-ROM

This is a basic guide for using the CD-ROM; for more detailed information please go to 'How to use the CD-ROM' on the start-up screen of the CD-ROM.

The CD-ROM contains resources for each book in the series. These might include: text extracts, differentiated text extracts, editable text extracts, photocopiable pages, interactive activities, images, videos, audio files, PowerPoint files, weblinks and assessment activities. There are also skeleton frames based on Sue Palmer's skeletons for teaching non-fiction text types. Also on the CD-ROM are the lesson notes for easy planning as Word file documents.

You can access resources in a number of ways:

Phase menu: The Phase menu provides all the resources used in that Phase. There are tabs at the top of the page denoting the resource type, for example 'Text'. If you click on this tab you will see a series of buttons to your left; if you press these then you will be taken to the other texts used within that Phase. You can print two versions of the text: either the screen – which shows any annotations made (see Whiteboard tools below) or Print PDF version, which will print an A4 size.

Resources menu: The resource menu lists every resource that is available on the CD-ROM. You can search by type of resource.

Whiteboard tools: This series contains a set of whiteboard tools. These can be used with any interactive whiteboard and from a computer connected to a projector. The tools available are: Hand tool – so that when you zoom in you can move around the screen; Zoom in; Zoom out; Pen tool for freehand writing or drawing; Highlighter; Line tool; Box tool; Text tool; Eraser tool; Clear screen; Hide annotations; Colour. You cannot save any changes made to the texts so always remember to 'Print Screen' when you annotate the CD-ROM pages.

Speak and listen for a range of purposes on paper and on screen strand checklist

	Narrative Unit 1	Narrative Unit 2	Narrative Unit 3	Narrative Unit 4	Narrative Unit 5	Narrative Unit 6	Non-fiction Unit 1	Non-fiction Unit 2	Non-fiction Unit 3	Poetry Unit 1	Poetry Unit 2	Poetry Unit 3
Strand 1 Speaking												
Telling a story using notes designed to cue techniques, such as repetition, recap and humour.	✔				✔							
Present a spoken argument, sequencing points logically, defending views with evidence and making use of persuasive language.						✔			✔			
Use and explore different question types and different ways words are used, including formal and informal contexts.								✔				
Strand 2 Listening and responding												
Identify different question types and evaluate impact on audience.		✔						✔				
Identify some different aspects of talk which vary between formal and informal occasions.				✔		✔	✔	✔	✔			
Analyse the use of persuasive language.									✔			
Strand 3 Group discussion and interaction												
Plan and manage a group task over time using different levels of planning.	✔					✔	✔				✔	
Understand different ways to take the lead and support others in groups.	✔					✔	✔	✔			✔	
Understand the process of decision making.	✔						✔	✔			✔	
Strand 4 Drama												
Reflect on how working in role helps to explore complex issues.		✔	✔		✔		✔	✔			✔	
Perform a scripted scene making use of dramatic conventions.		✔				✔						
Use and recognise the impact of theatrical effects in drama.						✔					✔	✔

Read for a range of purposes on paper and on screen strand checklist

	Narrative Unit 1	Narrative Unit 2	Narrative Unit 3	Narrative Unit 4	Narrative Unit 5	Narrative Unit 6	Non-fiction Unit 1	Non-fiction Unit 2	Non-fiction Unit 3	Poetry Unit 1	Poetry Unit 2	Poetry Unit 3
Strand 5 Word recognition												
Objectives covered by the end of Year 2.												
Strand 6 Word structure and spelling												
Spell words containing unstressed vowels.	✔	✔				✔					✔	
Know and use less common prefixes and suffixes, such as *im-, ir-, -cian*.	✔	✔		✔		✔		✔				
Group and classify words according to their spelling patterns and their meanings.	✔		✔			✔		✔			✔	
Strand 7 Understanding in interpreting texts												
Make notes on and use evidence from across a text to explain events or ideas.		✔						✔	✔	✔	✔	
Infer writers' perspectives from what is written and from what is implied.	✔		✔	✔	✔				✔	✔		✔
Compare different types of narrative and information texts and identify how they are structured.	✔	✔	✔		✔	✔	✔	✔	✔			
Use syntax, context and word structure to build their store of vocabulary when reading for meaning												
Distinguish between everyday use of words and their subject-specific use.												
Explore how writers use language for comic and dramatic effects.	✔	✔				✔			✔	✔	✔	✔
Strand 8 Engaging with and responding to texts												
Reflect on reading habits and preferences and plan personal reading goals.	✔		✔	✔				✔				
Compare the usefulness of techniques, such as visualisation, prediction, empathy, in exploring the meaning of texts.	✔	✔			✔		✔				✔	✔
Compare how a common theme is presented in poetry, prose and other genres.					✔	✔						✔

Write for a range of purposes on paper and on screen strand checklist

	Narrative Unit 1	Narrative Unit 2	Narrative Unit 3	Narrative Unit 4	Narrative Unit 5	Narrative Unit 6	Non-fiction Unit 1	Non-fiction Unit 2	Non-fiction Unit 3	Poetry Unit 1	Poetry Unit 2	Poetry Unit 3
Strand 9 Creating and shaping texts												
Reflect independently and critically on own writing and edit and improve it.		✔	✔	✔	✔	✔	✔	✔	✔	✔	✔	✔
Experiment with different narrative forms and styles to write their own stories.	✔	✔	✔		✔							
Adapt non-narrative forms and styles to write fiction or factual texts, including poems.				✔		✔	✔	✔		✔	✔	✔
Vary pace and develop viewpoint through the use of direct and reported speech, portrayal of action, selection of detail.			✔	✔			✔					
Create multi-layered texts, including use of hyperlinks, linked with web pages.							✔	✔	✔			
Strand 10 Text structure and organisation												
Experiment with the order of sections and paragraphs to achieve different effects.		✔	✔	✔		✔	✔	✔	✔			
Change the order of material within a paragraph, moving the topic sentence.							✔	✔	✔			
Strand 11 Sentence structure and punctuation												
Adapt sentence construction to different text-types, purposes and readers.	✔	✔	✔		✔	✔	✔	✔	✔			
Punctuate sentences accurately, including use of speech marks and apostrophes.		✔	✔	✔	✔	✔	✔	✔	✔			
Strand 12 Presentation												
Adapt handwriting for specific purposes, such as printing, use of italics.	✔	✔						✔		✔		✔
Use a range of ICT programs to present texts, making informed choices of which electronic tools to use for different purposes.		✔			✔	✔	✔	✔		✔	✔	✔

NARRATIVE
UNIT 1 Significant authors

Speak and listen for a range of purposes on paper and on screen

Strand 3 Group discussion and interaction
- Plan and manage a group task over time using different levels of planning.
- Understand different ways to take the lead and support others in groups.
- Understand the process of decision making.

Read for a range of purposes on paper and on screen

Strand 6 Word recognition: knowledge and skills
- Spell words containing unstressed vowels.
- Know and use less common prefixes and suffixes such as *im-, ir-, -cian*.
- Group and classify words according to their spelling patterns and their meanings.

Strand 7 Understanding and interpreting texts
- Infer writers' perspectives from what is written and what is implied.
- Compare different types of narrative and information texts and identify how they are structured.
- Explore how writers use language for comic and dramatic effects.

Strand 8 Engaging and responding to texts
- Reflect on reading habits and preferences and plan personal reading goals.
- Compare the usefulness of techniques such as visualisation, prediction and empathy in exploring the meaning of texts.

Write for a range purposes on paper and on screen

Strand 9 Creating and shaping texts
- Experiment with different narrative forms and styles to write their own stories.

Strand 11 Sentence structure and punctuation
- Punctuate sentences accurately, including using speech marks and apostrophes.
- Adapt sentence construction to different text-types, purposes and readers.

Strand 12 Presentation
- Adapt handwriting for specific purposes, for example printing, use of italics.

Progression in narrative

In this year, children are moving towards:
- Recognising that story structure can vary in different types of story and that plots can have high and low points; noticing that the structure in extended narratives can be repeated with several episodes building up to conflict and resolution before the end of the story; analysing more complex narrative structures and narratives that do not have a simple linear chronology, (such as parallel narratives, 'time slip').
- Developing particular aspects of story writing: experimenting with different ways to open the story; adding scenes, characters or dialogue to a familiar story; developing characterisation by showing the reader what characters say and do and how they feel and react at different points in the story.
- Planning and writing complete stories; organise more complex chronological narratives into several paragraph units relating to story structure; adapting for narratives that do not have linear chronology, such as portray events

▶

happening simultaneously (*Meanwhile...*); extending ways to link paragraphs in cohesive narrative using adverbs and adverbial phrases; adapting writing for a particular audience; aiming for consistency in character and style.

Key aspects of learning covered in this Unit

Evaluation
As they read and compare the work of particular authors, children will express and justify their judgements about books and about the author's style.

Enquiry
Children will decide how to answer questions about an author by using different sources of information, surveys of opinion, and so on.

Social skills
Children will participate in an extended group activity. They will take on a clearly defined role in the group, negotiate with others and reach agreement.

Self-awareness
Children will discuss and reflect on their personal responses to the texts.

Communication
Children will develop their ability to discuss as they work collaboratively in paired, group and whole-class contexts. They will communicate outcomes orally, in writing and through ICT if appropriate.

Prior learning

Before starting this Unit check that children can already:
■ Plan, tell and write complete stories with a clear sequence of events and showing how one event leads to another; use detailed description and powerful verbs to evoke setting and portray characters.
■ Participate in group discussion by offering reasons for their opinions supported by evidence, summarising ideas, reaching agreement and presenting ideas to an audience.
■ Talk about books by a favourite author, explaining why they enjoy them and how and why the books were written.
If they need further support please refer to a prior Unit or a similar Unit in Year 4.

Resources

Recommended class novel: *The Lottie Project* by Jacqueline Wilson; *Kensuke's Kingdom Extracts 1, 2* and *3* by Michael Morpurgo ❀; *Plane Crazy Parts 1* and *2* by Campbell Perry ❀; *The Lottie Project Extracts 1, 2* and *3* by Jacqueline Wilson ❀; *Michael Morpurgo biography Kensuke's Kingdom* ❀; Story mountain ❀; Photocopiable page 25 'Bones of a story'; Photocopiable page 26 'Top tips for story openings'; Photocopiable page 27 'Top tips for good dialogue'; Photocopiable page 28 'Tips for a great suspense paragraph!'; Interactive activity 'Charlie and George' ❀; Report skeleton ❀; Web links ❀; Photograph of the sea ❀; Audio of the sea ❀; Assessment activity 'Lost!'

Cross-curricular opportunities

History

UNIT 1 ■ Teaching sequence

Phase	Children's objectives	Summary of activities	Learning outcomes
1	I can identify how authors introduce characters and problems to a story. I can use empathy and visualisation to explore a text. I can identify the structure of a narrative . I can identify character's motivation and response using evidence from the text. I can compare openings to different texts, identifying similarities and differences. I can write own opening to a story.	Read *Plane Crazy* on CD-ROM. Identify problem, character and writer's style Use CD-ROM extracts to identify character's motivation and vocabulary. Use photocopiable page 25 to identify key elements to plot. Use Story mountain on CD-ROM to return to the structure of the story and to identify key moments in the story. Use CD-ROM extracts to identify good techniques for an opening to a story. Model own opening and children write opening using techniques identified	Children can understand how authors set up stories. Children can infer writer's perspectives. Children can structure of the story defined. Children can use empathy to identify character's motivation. Children know the features of a good opening to a story. Children can write an opening to a story applying features identified.
2	I can compare characterisation from evidence in text. I can identify how dialogue is used to convey character. I can identify how dialogue is used to convey character. I can learn to write dialogue accurately. I can write own new scene .	Use interactive activity from CD-ROM to compare characters from *The Lottie Project* and text extracts. Use Extract 2 *The Lottie Project* to identify dialogue and character. Refer to photocopiable page 27. Use Extract 3 *The Lottie Project* to demonstrate dialogue . Children improvise conversations. Children write own conversations. Children improvise a new scene. Children write own version of scene.	Children can infer about character's behaviour from text evidence. Children know and identify techniques for writing dialogue. Children can identify how dialogue is used in different ways in narrative. Children can write conversations using direct speech. Children can write dialogue between characters written in prose.
3	I can investigate and research two authors. I can punctuate complex sentences using commas. I can vary sentences to maintain reader's interest. I can deliver oral presentation on research of two authors.	Use author biographies to research information. Revise complex sentences and punctuation. Improve sentences by adding phrases, clauses, demarcating with commas . Create presentations on the two authors.	Children can make notes to answer questions about the author's life. Children can understand grammatical conventions for punctuating sentences. Children can vary sentences with different techniques to maintain interest. Children can use presentation skills to convey information.
4	I can identify how short sentences are used to create tension. I can write paragraphs using suspense. I can plan a short story based on own experience . I can write own story applying techniques learned. I can revise and edit own writing.	Use *Kensuke's Kingdom* extract 2 to identify how writers create tension. Children write paragraph based on own experience. Children create their own plans for a story. Children write their own story using the plans made, within a time limit. Children revise, edit and extend their writing in response to feedback.	Children know narrative techniques for creating tension. Children can write own paragraph applying knowledge from reading. Children can apply knowledge of structure of stories to own writing. Children can apply grammar and sentence-level work to writing. Children can revise a complete piece of writing.

Provide copies of the objectives for the children.

DAY 1 ■ Plane Crazy

Key features	Stages	Additional opportunities
Enquiry: identifying tricks the writer uses to engage the reader and maintain interest	**Introduction** Prior to starting this Unit of work read the short story *Plane Crazy* by Campbell Perry from the CD-ROM. Also read as a class novel *The Lottie Project* by Jacqueline Wilson and if time, *Kensuke's Kingdom* by Michael Morpurgo. Other books by both Michael Morpurgo and Jacqueline Wilson can be used as guided reading texts during this Unit. Explain to the children that over next four weeks they will look at how narrative is structured, organised, how openings are written and dialogue is laid out. The main objective of this lesson is to identify the tricks authors use to engage their readers and maintain interest.	
	Independent work Read *Plane Crazy Parts 1* and *2* with the children and then ask the following questions to identify the main teaching points: How does the author set up the characters and plot for the story? What aspects of the text show us what the main character is like? Why has the author chosen to write about this? Discuss and explain cultural and historical references. Provide children with copies of *Extract 1* and *Extract 2* and ask them to underline phrases in the text that provide evidence as to what the main character is like. Ask them to provide any evidence about the characters Birdy and Aunt Phyl.	**Extend:** provide a greater variety of tricks to highlight on their texts **Support:** provide clear prompts for text marking, for example *Underline everything the main character says*
	Plenary Discuss the children's work as a class and take feedback.	

DAY 2 ■ Writing a diary from Plane Crazy

Key features	Stages	Additional opportunities
Self awareness: using empathy to develop and deepen understanding of character's motivation and behaviour	**Introduction** Read *Plane Crazy Parts 1* and *2* from the CD-ROM and explore the plot and structure of the story. Then ask the following questions: How does the author show the main character's feelings? What techniques does the writer use to build up to the point of the building of the dam? Use hot-seating technique to find out how the main character feels about what he does to Aunt Phyl's kitchen.	If time, use this lesson to revise spelling patterns, for example doubling letters when *-ed* and *-ing* are added
	Independent work Ask the children to write a diary entry imagining themselves as the main character in the story, describing and justifying what he and Birdy do. Remind the children to use this as an opportunity to write in the first person. They could use the starting sentence: *I didn't mean to do it. I really didn't, but it just happened.*	**Extend:** provide a different starting line for the writing to the one in the lesson plan
	Plenary Discuss the story with the children. Do they think that the writer based this story on his own experience? If so, what evidence is there that it is? Invite the children to discuss similar experiences that they may have had, where they have been in trouble for something. Would they use these as the basis of their own stories later on? Children should record their ideas in their books for future reference. Then invite the children to read out their diary extracts.	**Support:** provide a frame with a speech bubble where the children can record the character's thoughts

DAY 3 ■ How is the Plane Crazy put together?

Key features	Stages	Additional opportunities
Enquiry: identify the structure of the story	**Introduction** Show the children the Story mountain from the CD-ROM. Explain that this represents how stories are usually structured, generally with a calm beginning, leading up to a climax (the highest point on the mountain) and then a finishing point. Ask the children to discuss which part of the mountain they think that *Plane Crazy Part 1* was from? Repeat this for *Plane Crazy Part 2*. They could then discuss which elements within the two extracts would fit on certain points on the mountain. **Independent work** Prepare copies of photocopiable page 25 'Bones of the Story' for one between two. Invite the children to sequence the story into the correct order of events. When they have done this ask them to look at the statements again to see if they can get rid of two statements that they believe are not essential and that without them, the story still makes sense. Repeat this until the children are down to six key statements that tell the essential parts of the story. **Plenary** As a class discuss the statements they discarded and what made them decide to eliminate them. Look at the statements they kept and look at where they would go on the Story mountain. Recap how all stories have a basic story structure to them.	when reading *The Lottie Project* at story time discuss with children how the structure of the story is different as there is a parallel story running through the book **Support:** provide TA support to the group if available in order to support the decision-making process

DAY 4 ■ Identify the key point in Plane Crazy

Key features	Stages	Additional opportunities
	Introduction Remind the children of the Story mountain and the basic story structure of *Plane Crazy*, identified using six essential statements. Recap briefly with the children how the statements were arrived at.	
Enquiry: identify character's motivation and response using evidence from the text	**Speaking and listening** Use the conscience alley technique to explore events at chosen points in the text. Divide the class into two lines. Choose one child to be the main character. Explain to children that one side of them are going voice the thoughts in the main character's head that tell him to make the dam while the other line is going to voice the thoughts in his head that tell him not to do it. As the child who is the main character from the story walks down the line, the children on either side voice the reasons for and against the action. Then discuss with the child acting as the main character which side was most persuasive. **Plenary** Reflect on how the technique helped the children to understand the character's motivation and feelings. Discuss also how the story might have changed if these events hadn't occurred.	**Extend:** invite children to think of an ending to the story if the key point had not taken place **Support:** direct focused, key questions to children so that they are all engaged and involved

DAY 5 ■ How do you write an opening to a story that grips the reader?

Key features	Stages	Additional opportunities
Evaluation: compare openings to different texts identifying similarities and differences	**Introduction** Explain to the children that they are going to compare the openings of different stories to find out what authors do to write effective openings. Briefly recap on the essential components of an opening: setting, character and problem. Use *Plane Crazy Part 1* and *Kensuke's Kingdom Extract 1* to compare ways that stories open. Use photocopiable page 26 'Top tips for story openings' as a reference for teaching points. Begin to make a list of the key features of a good opening: ■ Clear dramatic sentence, for example *I disappeared on the night before my twelfth birthday.* ■ Hook to interest the reader and make him or her read on. ■ Setting that is hinted at or suggested. ■ Characters introduced **Independent work** Provide children with copies of the extracts *Plane Crazy* and *Kensuke's Kingdom* and use the differentiated text *The Lottie Project Extract 1* (from the CD-ROM) for more confident learners. Ask the children to work in pairs to find some of the key features of a good opening that have been identified together as a class and see if they can identify some other techniques. **Plenary** Take feedback from groups to form a definitive list of key features of a good opening. Record this list on the board.	**Extend:** ask children to annotate text independently **Support:** provide children with key aspects of a good opening to identify

DAY 6 ■ Can you write an opening that grips the reader?

Key features	Stages	Additional opportunities
Communication: write own opening to a story using techniques identified	**Introduction** Remind the children of what they learned yesterday and explain that today they are going to try to apply their knowledge of how authors open stories to their own writing. Remind children of their ideas for their own stories that they discussed in the plenary on day 2. Explain that they are going to use these ideas as a starting point for writing their own openings to stories. Use paired talk to encourage children to talk about their ideas. Model for the children how to open a story making the teaching points identified. A starting point for this text could be: *I wanted it so badly. I really did, but I knew I would never get it. Everyone else in my class had one. I was the only one who didn't.* Show children how to apply what was taught yesterday to their own writing. Point out the importance of applying their understanding of punctuation of complex sentences. **Independent work** Ask the children to write their own openings, applying the techniques discussed and using their recorded ideas from the plenary in Phase 1, Day 2. **Plenary** Ask children to read their openings, inviting the others to see if they can pick out the techniques used from the list identified.	**Extend:** ask children to write their own story opening but provide them with a copy of the checklist so they can check off the features they have included **Support:** provide a short frame to support their writing

Guided reading

Use guided reading to further embed key teaching.

Focus on how the author introduces characters to the story. Encourage the children to make responses, justifying their comments with evidence from the text.

Use the opportunity in guided reading to discuss the structure of the text using a similar grid to the story mountain from the CD-ROM to chart the highs and lows of the key events in the story.

Assessment

From oral feedback and the quality of the discussions, monitor the children's progress in speaking and listening. Refer back to the learning outcomes on page 11.

Further work

Revise the use of the first and third person in narrative writing, Grammar for Writing Unit 14.

DAY 1 ■ What are characters like in different stories?

Key features	Stages	Additional opportunities
Evaluation: compare characters	**Introduction** Show the children the interactive activity 'Charlie and George' from the CD-ROM. Encourage the children to think of the differences between the two characters Charlie (from *The Lottie Project*) and George (from *Plane Crazy*). Drag and drop the correct descriptive words next to each character. When you have finished, encourage the children to point out evidence from the text which prove that these characters have these attributes.	
	Independent work Provide children with copies of *Plane Crazy Parts 1* and *2* and *The Lottie Project Extracts 2* and *3*. Ask children to identify the characteristics of each character by highlighting key words and phrases in the text to support their view. If children have read the whole story of *The Lottie Project* they may extended their knowledge of other characters in the text.	**Extend:** children write comparisons of characters **Support:** provide a small writing frame with sentence starters, for example *George is forgetful because*
	Plenary Ask children to summarise the characteristics of Charlie and George. Discuss briefly whether the writer allows them to change and grow over the duration of the story and how this is illustrated, for example Charlie's views of boys slowly changes as a result of a number of incidents.	

DAY 2 ■ How do authors use dialogue to show characters' feelings?

Key features	Stages	Additional opportunities
	Introduction Use *The Lottie Project Extract 2* to discuss how dialogue is used to show a character's feelings. Discuss how the writer shows a more compassionate side to Lottie through her actions and responses in the dialogue. Explain that the following points: when a new person speaks, the words they say are put on a new line, reporting clauses sometimes show the character is doing an action at the same time as speaking, punctuation marks are within speech marks Ask the following key questions: *How does the writer show Lottie's anxiety? How does Lottie manage to hide it from her mother?*	revise conventions of dialogue **Extend:** structure the text marking for children by giving them key things to find
Enquiry: identify how dialogue is used to convey character	**Independent work** Provide the children with *The Lottie Project Extract 2*. Ask less confident learners to identify the reporting clause and the speech of different people. Ask more confident learners to identify the way that the characters show what they are feeling Ask the children to complete photocopiable page 27 'Top tips for good dialogue'.	**Support:** create clear, specific prompts on the sheet, for example find three different reporting clauses
	Plenary Take feedback from the children using the photocopiable sheet. There should now be a class list of dialogue conventions and examples.	

DAY 3 ■ Dialogue and character opinion

Key features	Stages	Additional opportunities
Enquiry: identify how dialogue is used to convey character	**Introduction** Use *The Lottie Project Extract 3*. Identify how the dialogue and action show that Charlie's view of Jamie is changing. Use these questions: ■ *How does the conversation and incident show that Charlie's view of Jamie has changed?* ■ *How does the author show how Charlie reacts?* ■ *How does the author balance the conversation and the narration?* ■ *What clues do we, as the reader, get that Jamie likes Charlie?* Identify that the reporting clause varies. Sometimes it is just *said Charlie*, and at other times it has an action or description. Discuss how the author shows Charlie's internal thoughts through the narration and thus allows us, as readers, to gain insight into her thinking. Note that we know nothing about Jamie's views and thoughts, only his responses in relation to what Charlie notices about him. **Independent work** Model for children the use of adding prefixes and suffixes to root words to create new words. Use Spelling Bank pages 43 and 44 as reference material. **Plenary** Invite children to act out the scene between Charlie and Jamie. Then look for clues in the text about how they respond, look and talk to each other. These are the narration elements.	**Extend:** children learn words through syllabification **Support:** provide simple suffixes and prefixes that have a simple meaning Remind them that the root word can be spelt out with phonemes

DAY 4 ■ Writing dialogue

Key features	Stages	Additional opportunities
Communication: learn to write dialogue accurately	**Introduction** Explain the purpose of the lesson: to apply the techniques about writing dialogue that they have learned from reading to their own written conversations. **Speaking and listening** Use telephone conversations to rehearse dialogue orally. Provide children with a range of scenarios to stimulate discussions. Ask the children to pair up and then sit back to back so that they cannot see each other. Decide who is ringing who and what the conversation is. Refine the scenario so one of the children is persuading the other to agree to the proposal. Refer back to *The Lottie Project Extract 1* and discuss how you can show the differences in voice, tone and expression from the text and show it in the conversations. Ask children to revise their conversations with this in mind. **Independent work** Use one of the children's improvisations to model how to write the conversation down. As you write ask children to spot the techniques you are using to write. The children then write their own conversations. **Plenary** Children listen to each others conversations and identify the techniques used.	**Extend:** extend reporting clauses to include using and action, for example *replied John, as he picked up his book* **Support:** provide a simple frame to help children complete putting in speech marks

DAY 5 ▤ What would happen if characters from different stories met?

Key features	Stages	Additional opportunities
Communication: write own new scene with two main characters meeting	**Introduction** Recap the work done on Day 1 when characters from *Plane Crazy* and *The Lottie Project* were compared. Ask the children to discuss in pairs what these two characters would do if they met each other. Take feedback. **Speaking and listening** Discuss potential scenarios based on the text. Ask the children, in pairs, to improvise one of the scenes together. Watch the scenes and take feedback. Use one scenario as a stimulus for modelling how that character might tell the incident in a narrative. When modelling, recap on the conventions of dialogue. Show children how to balance direct and reported speech and narration to show us how what the character is thinking (see *The Lottie Project Extract 3*). **Independent work** Invite the children to write their own first person accounts of the new incident, either from the perspective of Charlie (therefore in the style of Jacqueline Wilson) or as the main character from *Plane Crazy*, in the style of Campbell Perry. **Plenary** Read out a few versions and invite children to comment on each others' work.	**Extend:** provide children with an opportunity to write as both main characters from each story **Support:** provide a simple writing frame for writing in the first person

Guided reading

In guided reading, point out the key aspects of dialogue that reinforce the techniques taught, for example action following conversation; sometimes no reporting clause; punctuation of sentences within dialogue.
Support children to make inferences about characters' behaviour and actions from evidence in the text.

Assessment

Assess the children's perceptions into character through the comments they make regarding the characters in this Phase.
Refer back to the learning outcomes on page 11.

Further work

Read a range of different books by Jacqueline Wilson and Michael Morpurgo. Are all the characters the same? Do the stories have similar themes running through them?

DAY 1 ◼ What makes an author want to write?

Key features	Stages	Additional opportunities
Enquiry: investigate and research two authors	**Introduction** Use the biography of Michael Morpurgo from the CD-ROM about *Kensuke's Kingdom*. You can also find biographies of Jacqueline Wilson and Michael Morpurgo on the internet to support the children's research into the two significant authors. Explain to the children that they are going to research the two authors with a view to creating a presentation about them at the end of the Phase. The children should think of questions that they would like to ask these authors about their life and writing. Using *Kensuke's Kingdom*, model how to skim and scan biographies to highlight and retrieve the answers to some of their questions. Record these on a KWL grid with the columns headed: *What do I know? What do I want to know? What I have learned.* Discuss how to record the important information by highlighting the answers to the question and then picking out the key words.	
	Independent work Provide children with copies of the research grid with the headings you have created and ask them to write down what they would like to find out about Michael Morpurgo or Jacqueline Wilson. They should then carry out their research and make notes. Make sure they keep copies of their notes and any web pages or texts they have used.	**Extend:** give the children biographies about other significant authors to practise note-taking
	Plenary Take feedback from the children regarding their research. Show the children how to categorise their information using the Report skeleton from the CD-ROM.	**Support:** provide a simple frame of key questions with answers in the text for them to locate

DAY 2 ◼ How are complex sentences punctuated?

Key features	Stages	Additional opportunities
Communication: punctuate complex sentences using commas	**Introduction** Revise the children's knowledge of complex sentences. Recap that a sentence is made up of a subject and a verb. Join two simple clauses together with *and*, for example *The sun was shining and the boy went down to the sea.* Identify the subject and verb in both clauses. Discuss the effect of the word *and*, and remind children that this is a compound sentence. Change the conjunction to *while* and discuss the effects. Provide a range of subordinating conjunctions and ask the children to write new sentences on their individual whiteboards. Discuss the use of the comma and its function. Refer to Grammar For Writing 34 for more activities and ideas.	
	Independent work Revisit the information about the authors researched yesterday. Provide groups of children with a copy of the Report skeleton from the CD-ROM. Ask them to group information that is similar. Encourage them to use this skeleton and the notes as a speaking tool to share information about their author.	**Extend:** provide relevant subordinating conjunctions, for example *while, as, if, when, since*
	Plenary Identify the key criteria for presentations, for example speaking loudly and clearly and everybody in the group taking a turn. Ask them to think about how to maintain the audience's interest during a presentation.	**Support:** provide simple conjunctions for example *and, so, but, when, because*

DAY 3 ◀ Improve writing by varying the types of sentences

Key features	Stages	Additional opportunities
Communication: vary sentence types to maintain readers' interest	**Introduction** Explain to the children that another way of maintaining the readers' interest is to vary the types of sentences used. Model three simple sentences together, followed by three different sentence types that say the same thing, for example *The boy stood on the stairs. He pulled his jumper out of his bag. He put it on.* *The boy, who was cross, stood on the stairs. Slowly, he pulled a jumper out of his bag. With a deep sigh, he put it on.* Discuss how the addition of a clause (sentence 1), the addition of an adverb (sentence 2), and the addition of a phrase (sentence 3) changes the rhythm and sound of the text. Discuss the use of commas to mark the clause, the phrase and the adverb. **Independent work** Let the children practise varying sentences using their own and other sentences. Differentiate the activity for some children so that they just add phrases and adverbs. **Plenary** Take feedback from children and discuss the improvements made. Show the children a new sequence of sentences. Discuss how they can be improved.	**Extend:** use relative clauses starting with *who* or *which* **Support:** provide a simple frame to help the children start each sentence differently

DAY 4 ◀ Why are Michael Morpurgo and Jacqueline Wilson important writers?

Key features	Stages	Additional opportunities
Social skills: prepare and deliver oral presentation on research of two authors	**Introduction** Show the children the Report skeleton from the CD-ROM. Explain that they are going to use the notes they made on Day 1 to form the basis of their group presentations on their choice of author. Model how to categorise the information from their notes onto the skeleton so there are four different aspects. Explain that the groups are going to present the information at the end of the lesson. **Speaking and listening** Provide the children with copies of the Report skeleton, they should also have their research notes and any web pages/extracts used. Allow children in their groups to assign roles for the task, categorise the information and prepare the presentation. Remind them that they can use props, books and extracts of texts if they want to enhance their presentations. Encourage them to rehearse orally. **Plenary** The groups present their presentations. Then discuss how effectively they worked together and how effective their presentations were in terms of voice, content and interest.	discuss the importance of collaboration and discussions and reaching a consensus in a group situation

Guided reading

Use guided reading sessions to discuss how the author varies sentence structures to maintain the interest of the reader.

Support children to make inferences about characters' behaviour and actions from evidence in the text.

Assessment

Observe the children as they work and ask them questions to check their understanding.

Refer back to the learning outcomes on page 11.

Further work

Use additional websites to further research the authors Michael Morpurgo and Jacqueline Wilson, for example http://www.booktrusted.co.uk/childrenslaureate/

Plan further work on the development of sentences.

DAY 1 ▪ Techniques to create tension

Key features	Stages	Additional opportunities
Enquiry: identify how short sentences are used to create tension	**Introduction** Use *Kensuke's Kingdom Extract 2* to discuss how writers create tension in their writing. To stimulate discussion and provide a context to the extract, use the image and the audio of the sea from the CD-ROM and discuss with children how they might feel if they fell into the sea. When reading the extract, explain that the author has used the following techniques to create tension: ■ the repetition of key words and phrases ■ the use of short sentences ■ the repetition of *I* ■ the build up of the sense of relief but it is a red herring. **Independent work** Provide some children with *Extract 2* and some with the differentiated text *Extract 3*. Ask children to underline all the techniques that create tension. They could write a list of these techniques. **Plenary** As a class, draw together the key points about writing suspense or tension and record these in a list for tomorrow's lesson. For example, ■ use short sentences to convey tension ■ hint at what it is that is frightening but don't tell the reader ■ use repeated phrases and words to create tension ■ use powerful verbs and precise adjectives to give clarity to the reader.	**Extend:** ask children to identify all areas listed independently without assistance **Support:** provide clear, specific directions to find information in the text, for example, *find and underline three short sentences*

DAY 2 ▪ Writing a suspense paragraph

Key features	Stages	Additional opportunities
	Introduction Discuss with the children real life experiences where they have felt tense, scared and frightened. Use one idea, for example walking in the wood, knowing something is following you to model a suspense paragraph. Use the following opening as a starting point *There was something behind me. I knew it. I could hear it. It was coming closer.* Draw the children into the writing by asking them to identify what techniques you are using, for example, short sentences, powerful verbs and so on. **Independent work** Give the children photocopiable page 28 'Tips for a great suspense paragraph!' to plan their own suspense paragraph. They should then write the paragraph in their books. Ask them to consider the context prior to writing, for example setting, characters and so on.	**Extend:** continue writing a second paragraph **Support:** provide a simple frame to support writing with a starting sentence, such as *It was behind me* Support children with a guided writing session
Communication: write own paragraph using techniques of suspense writing	**Plenary** Gather the children into a circle and invite individuals to read their paragraphs. The other children listen and then identify the techniques that have been used to create the tension.	

DAY 3 ■ Making a plan for a short story

Key features	Stages	Additional opportunities
Communication: plan own short story	**Introduction** Remind the children of the Story mountain they looked at from the CD-ROM in Phase 1 and jog their memories of how stories are structured. Explain to them that they are going to write a story in the first person where they want something and either tell a lie to get it or 'steal' or 'borrow' something. The story has to end with them being found out or resolving the bad thing they did themselves. **Speaking and listening** Ask the children to think of how the story will start, what the key events and climax will be, and then how it will finish. They need to think of setting and characters too. They should make notes. When the children have completed their notes, ask them to work in pairs to tell each other their ideas. Encourage them not just to read what they have written but to turn their pages over so that they retell their ideas. Invite the listeners to give feedback. **Plenary** Recap story structure with the class and invite the children to tell you their ideas. Give feedback on their ideas and planning.	**Extend:** children write detailed descriptions of what will happen in the story **Support:** allow children to use a planning frame to retell their story plan to another adult or child

DAY 4 ■ Writing the short story

Key features	Stages	Additional opportunities
Communication: write own story applying techniques	**Introduction** Start modelling writing your own story for the children. Remind the children that they need to engage the reader in the first few sentences of the text. Remind them that they need to think of how the paragraphs are organised. Invite the children to discuss the techniques you use as you write. Take the opportunity to reinforce the work covered on openings. Show the children how you are applying the use of dialogue and short sentences to create tension. Make explicit that you want the children to apply the following three aspects in their writing: an opening that hooks the reader in; dialogue that shows the difference between characters, and short sentences to convey tension. Recap the use of direct speech and how it is laid out. **Independent work** Ask the children to children use their own story planning notes from yesterday to write their story. Set an appropriate time limit for them to write their story. Leave your modelled text up on the board as a reference. This work will need written feedback to support the lesson on Day 5. **Plenary** Ask one or two children to read out their stories. Encourage the other children to give feedback. Then, in pairs, the children should read each others stories and choose one aspect of their partner's story that they think really shows how well they have written and discuss why this aspect is effective.	**Extend:** the children evaluate how good their story openings are against a checklist **Support:** provide a simple writing frame that will help the children structure their writing

DAY 5 ▪ Criticizing and improving writing

Key features	Stages	Additional opportunities

Evaluation: revise and edit own writing

Introduction
Much of this lesson relies on having given the children written feedback on their work from the previous day. Either use an extract of text written by one of the children or return to the text you modelled yesterday. Explain that all authors return to their texts after a break to re-read and refine their writing. Explain that they look for key things that make the writing precise: word choices, the order of the sentences, and the punctuation. Discuss with the children how they could improve one of the texts by changing any of the three areas identified. As decisions are made ask them to explain why the changes have made the writing better. For example, changing the word *walked* to *strolled* is better because the second word is more precise.

Independent work
Ask the children to return to their texts and choose one paragraph to rewrite, looking for ways to improve it. Structure the activity by providing a sequence of things to do:
- read the paragraph, underlining any weak words or phrases
- look again, this time at punctuation, is there anything you have missed out?
- look again at the word order, have you started your sentences the same way, for example *Then I..., Then I...?*

Plenary
Invite the children to read their paragraphs to each other, explaining their changes. Take feedback.

Extend: structure the redrafting process by providing criteria that they have to improve, for example relative clauses, varied sentence starters and short sentences

Support: structure redrafting to look for punctuation, variety of connectives, interesting vocabulary

Guided reading
Support children to make inferences about characters' behaviour and actions from evidence in the text.

Assessment
Use the assessment sheet 'Lost!' from the CD-ROM to assess how far the children have applied the different aspects of narrative covered in the Unit.
Refer back to the learning outcomes on page 11.

Further work
Stimulate further discussion about the structure of narrative writing.
Reinforce key aspects of adding suffixes and prefixes to words.

Bones of the story

■ Cut out the bones of the story and put them in the correct order.

✂

We got to Great Aunt Phyl's gate when Birdy suggested buliding a dam on the stream to bomb.
Birdy and I apologised, Great Aunt Phyl took us to see what we had caused.
Great Aunt Phyl came in, she seemed rather cross.
We flew back home, but Mum got annoyed at us pretending to be planes. She sent us to tell Great Aunt Phyl when tea would be ready.
The whole of downstairs was under water and mud.
We didn't get to Great Aunt Phyl's.
There was no real damage done, we laughed about it later.
Mum asked where Great Aunt Phyl was, I'd forgotten.
She complained about someone damming up her stream, her house was flooded.
Great Aunt Phyl asked us to be mud busters and to clean up the mess.
Great Aunt Phyl, Birdy and I went to see 'The Dam Busters' on my eighth birthday.
We made the dam, but before we could find any bombs, Mum shouted "teatime".

NARRATIVE ■ UNIT 1

Top tips for story openings

■ Write the key features of a good story opening below. Two top tips have been given to you to start you off.

Top tips for writing a really interesting opening to a story.

✔ Start with a dramatic opening sentence.

✔ Suggest where the story takes place by giving a clue, for example 'Sarah looked in her wardrobe for her clothes'.

✔ _____

_____

_____

✔ _____

_____

_____

✔ _____

_____

_____

✔ _____

_____

_____

■ 100 LITERACY FRAMEWORK LESSONS YEAR 5

Top tips for good dialogue

■ From the work you have done, add to the list below some good tips for writing dialogue in stories. Provide an example to illustrate each tip.

Top tips for writing good dialogue.

✔ Make sure what your character says is inside the speech marks.

Example: _____

✔ Put any question marks and explanation marks and commas inside the speech marks.

Example: _____

✔ _____

_____

Example: _____

✔ _____

_____

Example: _____

✔ _____

_____

Example: _____

✔ _____

_____

Example: _____

Tips for a great suspense paragraph!

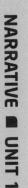 Use this page to plan your suspense paragraph. Don't forget to look at the tips at the bottom of the page.

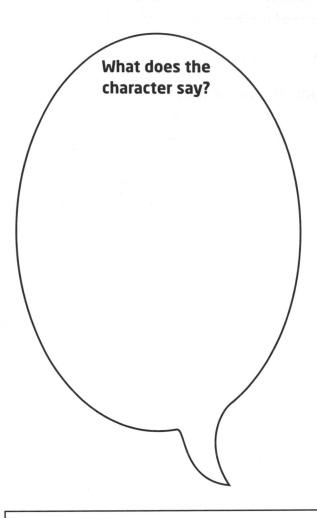

What does the character say?

> What is the setting or situation?

> Which characters are there?

> Think of words to describe the scene.

Tips for writing a great suspense paragraph!

(Remember to add your own.)

- Use short sentences.
- Repeat certain words and phrases.
- Show the reader what your character is thinking by using questions.
- Use powerful verbs and precise adjectives to give the reader a clear picture of what is happening.

_____

_____

_____

_____

NARRATIVE
UNIT 2 Traditional stories, myths and legends

Speak and listen for a range of purposes on paper and on screen

Strand 1 Speaking
- Tell a story using notes designed to cue techniques, such as repetition, recap and humour.

Strand 2 Listening and responding
- Identify different question types and evaluate their impact on the audience.

Strand 4 Drama
- Reflect on how working in role helps to explore complex issues.
- Perform a scripted scene making use of dramatic conventions.

Read for a range purposes on paper and screen

Strand 6 Word structure and spelling
- Spell words containing unstressed vowels.
- Know and use less common prefixes and suffixes, such as *im-, ir-, -cian.*

Strand 7 Understanding and interpreting texts
- Make notes on and use evidence from across a text to explain events.
- Compare different types of narrative and information texts and identify how they are structured.
- Explore how writers use language for comic and dramatic effects.

Strand 8 Engaging with and responding to texts
- Compare the usefulness of techniques such as visualisation, prediction and empathy in exploring the meaning of texts.

Write for a range of purposes on paper and screen

Strand 9 Creating and shaping texts
- Reflect independently and critically on their own writing and edit and improve it.
- Experiment with different narrative forms and styles to write own stories.

Strand 10 Text structure and organisation
- Experiment with the order of sections and paragraphs to achieve different effects.

Strand 11 Sentence structure and punctuation
- Adapt sentence construction to different text types, purposes and readers.
- Punctuate sentences accurately, including using speech marks and apostrophes.

Strand 12 Presentation
- Adapt handwriting for specific purposes, for example printing, use of italics.
- Use a range of ICT programs to present texts, making informed choices about which electronic tools to use for different purposes.

Progression in narrative

In this year, children are moving towards:
- Comparing the structure and features of different versions of the same story, for example retellings from different times or countries, adaptations for different age-groups. Noting repeated patterns of events – climax- resolution in extended narratives.
- Identifying the audience that the author had in mind for a particular story.
- Exploring how narration relates to events.

▶

UNIT 2 ◄ Traditional stories, myths and legends *continued*

■ Looking for evidence of characters changing during a story and discussing possible reasons, what it shows about the character and whether the change met or challenged children's expectations.
■ Reviewing features of typical settings for different types of traditional story. Identifying examples of effective description which evoke time or place.

Key aspects of learning covered in this Unit

Enquiry
Children will investigate a range of narrative texts by asking relevant questions and research and then plan and present these narratives orally and in writing.

Creative thinking
Children will generate and extend imaginative ideas to create a narrative. They will suggest hypotheses, responding imaginatively through drama and talk, and respond to problems in order to create a written outcome.

Information processing
Children will identify relevant information from a range of sources on paper and on screen and use this to present orally and write their own legends.

Reasoning
Children will draw inferences and make deductions to clarify, extend and follow up ideas in their oral and written work.

Evaluation
Children will present information orally, through drama and in writing. They will discuss success criteria, give feedback to others and judge the effectiveness of their own work.

Communication
Children will develop their skills to reflect critically on what they have seen and read. They will develop their ability to present a narrative for different audiences orally and in writing and reflect critically on their own and others' work.

Prior learning

Before starting this Unit check that the children can:
■ Identify features of different genres of fiction texts.
■ Comment on performances, discussing effects and how they are achieved.
■ Plan, tell and write complete stories with a clear sequence of events and showing how one event leads to another.
■ Organise texts into paragraphs.
If they need further support please refer to a prior Unit or a similar Unit in Year 4

Resources

Arthur High King of Britain by Michael Morpurgo ✎; *Pandora's box Extracts 1 and 2* by Campbell Perry ✎; Text and audio file of *Jason and the Golden Fleece* by Campbell Perry ✎; Story mountain ✎; Interactive activity 'Match it!' ✎; Web links ✎; Picture of Jason and the Golden Fleece ✎; Photocopiable page 44 'Bones of the story – Pandora's box'; Photocopiable page 45 'Bones of the story – Garden of Eden'; Photocopiable page 46 'Creation stories'; Photocopiable page 47 'Pandora's justification'; Photocopiable page 48 'Story framework'; Assessment activity 'Quest for the Golden Owl's Claw' ✎

Cross-curricular opportunities

History

UNIT 2 ■ Teaching sequence

Phase	Children's objectives	Summary of activities	Learning outcomes
1	I can identify the key features of a myth through reading. I can explore how the writer uses language for drama. I can compare different versions of similar stories.	Tell the stories of the *Garden of Eden* and *Pandora's Box*. Use photocopiable pages. Use *Pandora's Box* to identify language effects. Compare versions of *Pandora's Box*. Compare *Pandora's Box* with *Garden of Eden*.	Children can recognise the features of a myth. Children can identify and explain language effects. Children can compare and contrast two different stories.
2	I can compare the structure of similar stories. I can understand how empathy and working in role can explore complex issues. I can identify key parts of the story and characters' motivations. I can make notes and use evidence from the text to justify ideas. I can revise work on dialogue rules and conventions. I can work in role and use different narrative forms. I can experiment with the order of paragraphs in writing.	Identify similarity in structure of *Pandora's Box* and *Garden of Eden*. Use CD-ROM extracts, hot-seating and role play to identify similarities and differences between characters. Read *Pandora's Box* extract from CD-ROM to identify different characters' thoughts and feelings at key points in the story. Use *Pandora's Box* extracts from CD-ROM. Interview Pandora using photocopiable page to make notes and to plan letter-writng. Turn examples of direct speech into reported speech. Children write own letters from Pandora to the God Zeus. Children re-order a paragraph in Pandora's letter to improve her argument.	Children can identify the structure of the myth. Children can work in role to discuss another character's motivations. Children can work in role to discuss another character's motivations. Children can use evidence from the text to justify views. Children can understand the difference between direct and reported speech. Children can write a letter in role as Pandora justifying her actions. Children can see how paragraph order can affect the reader.
3	I can compare audio and written versions of myths. I can compare auditory and written versions of the text. I can identify good language features from texts read. I can plan a retelling of known myth using oral techniques. I can retell a known myth using oral techniques.	Listen to *Jason and the Golden Fleece* on CD-ROM. Children choose an extract from *Pandora's Box* to tell orally. Read *Arthur High King of Britain* on CD ROM. Children create short auditory versions. Use CD-ROM extracts to create a list of effective words and phrases. Children create own version of a known myth. Children prepare the telling. Children in pairs or threes retell own version of a known myth.	Children can identify the difference between oral and written myths. Children can identify features of oral and written versions. Children can list good storytelling words and phrases. Children can plan their own version of a myth. Children can retell a known myth in a group, using oral techniques.
4	I can identify the characteristics of heroes. I can plan my own myth using modelled strategies. I can write myths. I can reflect critically on my own writing. I can write myths.	Revise spellings of common prefixes. Planning of their mythical hero. Children create their own plan of a myth. Children begin to write their own myth using language features. Children select a paragraph and edit and improve their own writing. Children complete their writing of their own myth.	Children can identify the characteristics of their mythical hero. Children can plan their own myth/story. Children can begin to write their own myth. Children can edit and improved their writing. Children can complete their stories.

Provide copies of the objectives for the children.

DAY 1 ◀ What are the features of a myth?

Key features	Stages	Additional opportunities
Enquiry: identify the key features of a myth through reading	**Introduction** Discuss with the children what they understand by the term *traditional tale*. Discuss some examples, such as *The Hare and the Tortoise*. What was the key message in this story? (It doesn't pay to cheat.) What other traditional stories do the children know? For example, *King Arthur and the Knights of the Round Table; Robin Hood*. Discuss the content and how they might have originated, for example Arthur based on fact and the story changed over time. *The Hare and the Tortoise* is a Greek fable that carries a message. Explain that the Unit is going to cover myths in some detail to link with Greek work. **Independent work** Provide children with photocopiable page 44 'Bones of the story Pandora's box' and page 45 'Bones of the story Garden of Eden'. Explain that these are two creation stories that have been chopped up into sections. Ask children in pairs to sequence each of the stories in the order that they think makes sense so that they have a clear chronology of events in the two stories. **Plenary** Gather the children together and discuss what the stories' sequence of events were. Discuss the children's ideas of what a myth is. Ask the children to identify whether any of the characteristics are in the stories they sequenced. Clarify with children different definitions of myths, legends and fables: 1 A traditional story based on real events but changed over time. 2 A traditional story with heroes and gods that explain how things occurred.	see the web links from the CD-ROM for more examples of myths and traditional stories

DAY 2 ◀ What did Pandora do?

Key features	Stages	Additional opportunities
Enquiry: explore how the writer uses language for dramatic effect	**Introduction** Read *Pandora's Box Extract 1* with the children and discuss the author's use of language to describe the different characters, setting and narrator voice. Focus particularly on the how the writer shows Pandora's curiosity about the box. Through shared reading, identify the different techniques the author has used to show the characters of Epimetheus and Pandora. Discuss the effects of the choice of vocabulary on the reader. Explore how the text would sound with different adjectives or phrases that are less powerful. Ask the children to discuss the images the words create in their heads as they are reading them. **Independent work** Provide children with copies of the extract. Ask them to underline all the words or phrases that describe the box; find three phrases that show what Epimetheus is feeling; find five examples that show that Pandora is curious about the box. **Plenary** Return to the text and discuss with the whole class the details the author uses to show how the box tempts her. Record or highlight these on the text.	differentiate the work by changing the types of language features you are asking the children to identify **Support:** be specific about features you want them to identify, for example three things Pandora says

DAY 3 ■ Compare different versions of story

Key features	Stages	Additional opportunities
	Introduction Use *Pandora's Box Extract 1* and a version of the story from the internet, such as http://atschool.eduweb.co.uk/carolrb/greek/pandora.html as source material for this lesson. Read the version shown on the internet and discuss the similarities and differences between the two versions. Create a chart on a board or flipchart to record observations; use the following headings: *Background to the story; Story-telling techniques; Insight into characters' feelings and motivation; Use of descriptive language; Events of the story.* Discuss with the children the different purposes of the stories and why the writers might have emphasised different parts. Record these observations onto the chart.	
Enquiry: compare different versions of the same story	**Independent work** Return the children to their sequenced versions of *Pandora's Box* and the *Garden of Eden* (Day 1, Independent work). Provide them with copies of the grid on photocopiable page 46 'Creation stories', on which they should record their observations about the similarities and differences between these two stories. The categories are: the setting, the characters, the temptation, the consequence of the action, the reason that Pandora and Eve were created. Remind children to record their details in as full sentences as possible.	**Extend:** practise spelling words with stressed and unstressed vowels
Communication: contribute to class discussion	**Plenary** Conduct a whole-class discussion where the children identify and explain the comparisons they have made. *What are the common themes between the two?* Record the children's ideas on a flipchart, using the following categories: settings, characters, main events, ending. Discuss the similarities and differences the children have noted.	**Support:** modify photocopiable page 46 to suit the ability of the children

Guided reading
Read a number of different Greek myths, for example *Theseus and the Minotaur*, *Jason and the Golden Fleece*.
Discuss and add any additional features that these myths show, for example characters are superheroes; they often have to carry out tasks to prove themselves before getting the prize. Discuss settings and contexts for these texts.

Assessment
Monitor children's understanding of the features of myths through whole-class discussion and oral contributions as well as through marking the children's work, for example comparison grid, and language features annotated.
Refer back to the learning outcomes on page 31.

Further work
Read aloud *Arthur High King of Britain* by Michael Morpurgo explaining that this is a legend – it is based upon some truth that over the years has changed. Discuss common characteristics that the legend has with a myth, for example superhero character, magic sword and so on.
For homework, ask children to research facts about Robin Hood and King Arthur.

DAY 1 ▪ How are myths structured?

Key features	Stages	Additional opportunities
Enquiry: compare and identify the structure of similar stories	**Introduction** Use photocopiable page 44 'Bones of the story Pandora's Box' to help children identify the structure of the story in pairs. Copy enough of the sheet and cut each statement into a strip so each pair has a set. Ask the children to reduce the statements by two so that the story still makes sense as they read the statements together. Repeat this each time so that eventually each pair is left with six statements that tell the bare essence of the story. Discuss with the children their decisions for discarding certain statements and how the ones that remain are really relevant. Use the Story mountain from the CD-ROM to discuss with the children how the statements could be organised in height so that they reflect the differing levels of interest, excitement and tension of the story.	**Extend:** children draw their own story mountain for the six statements deciding which is the most exciting
Reasoning: class discussion	**Independent work** Ask the children to repeat the activity for photocopiable page 45 'Bones of the story Garden of Eden'. Print copies of the Story mountain for the children to refer to. **Plenary** Discuss the different statements and levels that the *Garden of Eden* story has and how it is similar to the *Pandora's Box*. Can the children do the same for other myths that they have read?	**Support:** provide the statements for another story to sort and discard

DAY 2 ▪ What do Pandora and Epimetheus think?

Key features	Stages	Additional opportunities
Evaluation: exploring the text	**Introduction** Return to *Pandora's Box Extract 1* and re-read it with the class, this time focusing on the differences between the characters and their relationships with each other. In the text look for key differences between the characters, for example *Epimetheus explained patiently* – the adverb *patiently* tells the reader how he is feeling about Pandora.	play spelling games that reinforce spelling patterns and rules, for example doubling letters, rules for adding -*ed* and -*ing*
	Speaking and listening Explain to the children that they are going to interview the two characters Epimetheus and Pandora. Encourage them to think of the types of questions that they might want to ask. Choose two children to be the characters and conduct the interview.	**Extend:** encourage the children to think of different question types
Creative thinking: understand how empathy and working in role can explore complex issue	**Independent work** Set up paired role play for the children where they explore the conversation and behaviour between the two characters the morning after Pandora has opened the box. Encourage the children to develop a small piece of dialogue that develops the characters and shows their feelings **Plenary** Read with the children *Pandora's box Extract 2* and look for clues that show the relationship between the two characters.	**Support:** provide key questions for the children to ask in role play

DAY 3 ■ Why did Pandora do it?

Key features	Stages	Additional opportunities
Reasoning: identify key parts of the story and characters' motivation	**Introduction** Read *Pandora's box Extract 2* with the children – the point where Pandora opens the box. Discuss how the writer shows that the box is irresistible to Pandora, for example the use of rhetorical questions, the description of the box's behaviour and so on. Remind the children of the Story mountain from the CD-ROM and to identify which part of the story structure this extract is from. Then ask: *What are Pandora's choices? How do we know that her need to open the box is greater than her need to obey Epimetheus?*	
Creative thinking: practical group work	**Speaking and listening** Explain to the children that they are going to explore Pandora's thoughts at two key moments in the story. One just before she opens the box and one at the point when the box is open. Use the conscience alley method. Divide the children in two lines; choose one child to be Pandora; explain that one line is going to voice all the thoughts that tell her she has to open the box, while the other is going to voice all the thoughts that tell her not to. Encourage the children to think carefully about their contributions, referencing them from within the story.	**Extend:** ask children to write sentences about how the characters are feeling **Support:** involve children in conscience alley by reminding them they can repeat a thought or question
	Plenary Recap Pandora's thoughts as a class. Then briefly discuss what Epimetheus might think when he sees the box open. Discuss how the relationship between Pandora and Epimetheus might have changed.	

DAY 4 ■ Planning a letter from Pandora

Key features	Stages	Additional opportunities
	Introduction Provide children with copies of *Pandora's box Extracts 1 and 2* and discuss whether Pandora was right to do what she did. Remind the children what the world was like prior to the box being opened and what it was like after. Have a brief discussion about what the effect of letting Hope out of the box might have and how it changed things. Use the two texts to track Pandora's thoughts through the text. Does she feel responsible for what she did? Is there any evidence for her regretting it? Briefly make notes of the board to show what her thoughts are.	
Information processing: to make notes and use evidence from the text to justify ideas	Explain to the children that they are going to re-interview Pandora to discuss how she justifies what she has done. In pairs, ask the children to think of questions to ask. They should record these on their individual whiteboards. Discuss briefly how they may have to ask an open question first and then a follow-up question to get the answer they want. Then ask the children to carry out the interview in their pairs, with one child acting as Pandora.	**Extend:** children use expanded reasons in their notes explaining Pandora's thoughts
	Independent work Explain to the children that they are going to write a letter from Pandora to the Gods, explaining and justifying what she did. They are going to plan this today and write the letter another day. She is going to argue that she was right. Children should plan the letter using photocopiable page 47 'Pandora's justification'. They will write the letter on Day 6.	**Support:** provide a simpler version of photocopiable page 47 with prompts
	Plenary As a class discuss Pandora's reasons for what she did. Take and give feedback.	

DAY 5 ▪ Direct and reported speech

Key features	Stages	Additional opportunities
Communication: understand how to change direct speech to reported speech	**Introduction** Revise the use of direct and reported speech. Use examples from *Pandora's box Extract 1* to show children how to change to direct speech to reported speech. For example *"Close your eyes!" he commanded* (direct); *Zeus commanded Epimetheus and Prometheus to close their eyes* (reported). Discuss the difference between the two forms with the children – one being the character's voice, the other more the voice of a narrator. **Independent work** Provide children with a number of different examples of direct speech and ask them to turn these into reported speech. They should identify each time which words they have used to turn it to reported speech, for example *she said that...* **Plenary** Return to *Pandora's Box Extract 2* and show what effect turning the direct speech to reported speech has on the narrative. Explain that it is better to have a balance between the two types of speech.	revise the rules for punctuating dialogue **Extend:** provide opportunities to change reported speech into direct speech **Support:** support the children to turn direct speech into reported speech orally

DAY 6 ▪ Pandora's letter

Key features	Stages	Additional opportunities
Information processing: to experiment with different narrative forms	**Introduction** Using the notes made on photocopiable page 47 remind the children of the key points for Pandora's justification for what she did. Stress the importance of making a key point and then elaborating on it. Explain that they are going to write the letter from Pandora to the God Zeus arguing that she was right to open the box. Use shared writing to model part of the letter to the children. As you write, ask the children to identify key aspects of the narrative you have drawn on to enhance the argument, for example: the strength of the box pulling her to do it, hope being released and so on. Show the children how paragraphs can enhance and structure the writing. Draw attention to how the voice of Pandora can come through the letter, for example defiant. Discuss how punctuation can help the writer convey how she feels. Model the use of reported speech. **Independent work** Ask the children to have a go at writing their own version of Pandora's justification, applying the teaching points used in the modelled session. **Plenary** Invite the children to read their letters to each other, discussing any writing they think is effective. Ask them to focus on identifying the structure of the letter so that Pandora makes her point and then elaborates upon it.	**Extend:** provide a list of criteria for the children to check in their writing, for example connectives, expansion on reasons, consistent first person and so on **Support:** provide a structured writing frame for support in letter writing

DAY 7 ■ How can a paragraph be written more effectively?

Key features	Stages	Additional opportunities
	### Introduction Use an example of the children's text to discuss the order of the points made in the letter by Pandora. Show the children how by rearranging the paragraphs as a starting point the text can convey a different argument and create a different strength. Deepen the discussion with the children by showing them how to write a paragraph where the sentences develop and extend an idea. Show children how each sentence in a paragraph can start in a different way.	revise and consolidate the use of commas within sentences
Reasoning: to experiment with the order and sections of paragraphs in writing	### Independent work Ask the children to return to the letter from Pandora that they wrote yesterday. They should choose a paragraph that they feel they have not developed enough and rewrite it, using the ideas modelled in whole-class sessions.	**Extend:** children revise work to publication standard and produce for display
	### Plenary Choose children to read their revised paragraphs, identifying the changes. Encourage them to identify which paragraph now presents the strongest argument from Pandora justifying what she's done.	**Support:** provide a paragraph with each sentence cut up for children to reorder

Guided reading
Use guided reading sessions to focus on the portrayal of characters in different myths.
Discuss with the children how the writer has used direct and reported speech to enhance and balance the writing.

Assessment
Informally assess the children's progress in speaking and listening by identifying their ability to empathise, express ideas in extended sentences and use their knowledge of the text, characters and events in their justifications. Refer to the learning outcomes on page 31.

Further work
Continue to revise work on the addition of prefixes and suffixes to root words. Develop the use of spelling journals where children record and learn spellings that they are making.

DAY 1 ▇ Is a myth different when you hear it?

Key features	Stages	Additional opportunities
Enquiry: compare audio and written versions of myths	### Introduction Tell the children that myths are embedded in an oral tradition of storytelling and that different versions of the story will have different events and will emphasise different things. Listen to the audio of *Jason and the Golden Fleece* from the CD-ROM. Then read the text version from the CD-ROM and discuss the difference between the two. Discuss the visual pictures that children get in their heads as a result of listening, for example what does Jason look like? What is the ship he is sailing like? Ask the children to note their ideas. Show the children the image from the CD-ROM and listen to the audio file again. Ask the children: *Is Jason the same as the picture you had of him in your heads?* Talk about some of the storytelling techniques that have been used on the audio version, for example difference in tone of voice. Explain to the children that this myth has a superhero who has to complete tasks. ### Independent work Provide the children with copies of the two extracts of *Pandora's Box* from the CD-ROM. Ask them, in pairs, to choose an extract and rehearse orally how they would tell the story as if for radio. Ask them to identify where they would change their voices and add sound effects. Remind the children that the story they tell can be different to the extract. A written story can't be changed, but in oral retelling it can be altered. Make it clear to the children they can change the order of some of the events because they are telling the story aloud. ### Plenary Choose some of the children to tell their excerpt of *Pandora's Box* using voice and sound effects.	discuss clues in the text to tell you what expressions to use. Link to dialogue – reporting clauses **Extend:** put together a prompt sheet of main events with one word as a prompt for story telling **Support:** provide a set of key things children need to include in their oral storytelling, for example gestures, tone of voice and so on

DAY 2 ▇ How does a writer tell a story?

Key features	Stages	Additional opportunities
Enquiry: compare audio and written versions of the text	### Introduction Show the children the extract *Arthur High King of Britain* by Michael Morpurgo from the CD-ROM. Discuss how the writer introduces the character and what devices he uses to set up the retelling of the legend. (Children should be familiar with this text if it has been read as a class novel and at this point in the Unit, will be familiar with the story and events.) Provide the children with copies of the extract and ask them, in pairs, to identify some of the language effects that the author uses to introduce the reader to the main character. What hooks has the writer put in to make you wonder what is going on? Discuss with the children which parts of the extract they would use to turn this version into an audio version.	
	### Independent work Ask the children in groups or pairs to decide how to create a short audio version of the scene. Ensure that they have a narrator voice and create sound effects.	**Extend:** encourage the children to listen to other audio versions of stories and discuss effects **Support:** provide a list of clues of what to look out for in an audio version of a story
Communication: presenting audio stories	### Plenary Listen to some of the children's versions and recap the key differences between audio and written versions.	

DAY 3 ■ Language and good storytelling

Key features	Stages	Additional opportunities
Enquiry: collect and identify good language features from texts read	**Introduction** Explain to the children that all good writers have learned about effective words and phrases from texts they have read. Use the extracts *Arthur High King of Britain* and *Pandora's Box Extracts 1* and *2* from the CD-ROM to identify effective words and phrases with the children by highlighting them. Discuss with the children what made the words effective and what images or pictures they create in the reader's mind.	revise some work linked to complex sentences and punctuation
	Independent work Ask the children to create their own list of good storytelling words and phrases from the text extracts from the CD-ROM or from other texts that they are currently reading. The children should then categorise the words and phrases that describe characters' actions and feelings at certain points in the story. Ask them to look for connectives that join paragraphs and events together.	**Extend:** provide a series of phrases from the texts so that the children can explain why they are effective
Communication: verbal communication and explanation	**Plenary** Discuss the lists with the children, encouraging them to identify and explain why they chose particular words and phrases. Create a list of the best words and phrases on a flipchart or whiteboard for use in writing later.	**Support:** provide phrases to sort into categories

DAY 4 ■ Plan a retelling of a myth

Key features	Stages	Additional opportunities
	Introduction Explain that the children are going to work in groups to create an oral retelling of one of the myths they have become familiar with: *Pandora's Box, Jason and the Golden Fleece,* or *King Arthur.* Tell them that they are going to create a script and that it must be for an audio version only (no acting).	link back to work on scripting plays, Greek theatres and use of masks
Creative thinking: plan retelling of a known myth using techniques such as repetition, recap and humour	**Speaking and listening** Divide the children into groups of four. They will need to appoint roles so that the story can be divided up into parts, for example two of them work on the first part of writing the scripts – including the sound effects – while the other two work on another part of the story. Start the children off by giving them photocopiable page 49 'Story framework' where they can note down the key moments prior to dividing up the roles and parts of the story. By the end of the lesson they should have drafted the story, decided on sound effects and how they are going to create them, and allocated parts of characters to different voices. They need to have the scripts for the different scenes identified.	**Extend:** ask the children to write a list of what constitutes a good script **Support:** provide a script outline and a specific scene for children to retell orally
	Plenary Invite a group of four to share their work so far. Encourage feedback and whole-class discussion.	

DAY 5 ▪ Performing an oral storytelling of a myth

Key features	Stages	Additional opportunities
Creative thinking: retell known myth using oral techniques such as recap, repetition and humour	**Introduction** Explain to the children that they are going to refine and rehearse their oral versions of the myths. Explain that during this session, they need to clarify: ■ the script ■ the roles people are taking ■ the sound effects being used ■ which section comes first. Remind them that they are not expected to retell the whole story but just four stages of it (two stages written by one pair in the group, two stages written by the other). Encourage the children to create as many sound effects as they can by using their voices.	
	Independent work Provide the children with time to rehearse and refine their performances. Give them a time limit by which they need to have finished discussing and move on to rehearsing their work. If possible, give them time to record their oral versions using an ICT programme that creates sound files.	**Extend:** use ICT to create an MP3 file of the stories
Evaluation: evaluating group work as a class	**Plenary** Display some examples of the children's scripts onto a whiteboard or projector so that you can evaluate how effective their directions were. Listen to their performance first then show the script (and the audio track if available) concurrently and evaluate the usefulness of the script that they created. Repeat with other groups' work.	**Support:** provide a simple structure for the children to write their script

Guided reading
Use guided reading to continue to work on developing the children's ability to make inferences from the text.
Discuss the authors' vocabulary and word choices and their effects.

Assessment
Informally assess children's progress in speaking and listening, identifying their ability to negotiate, work together, listen, collaborate and perform.
Refer back to the learning outcomes on page 31.

Further work
From analysis of the children's writing, identify the key areas of weakness in spelling and teach the key rules.
Some areas are:
■ rules for doubling letters when -ed and -ing are added
■ syllabification.

DAY 1 — Devise mythical characters for your own Greek myth

Key features	Stages	Additional opportunities
Creative thinking: devise own mythological characters	**Introduction** Revise the rules for adding less common prefixes and suffixes and the rules for adding suffixes. Explain to the children that over the next two lessons they are going to plan and devise their own myths which include a quest theme and challenges for the hero. Discuss the key aspects of different ancient Greek super heroes, for example Jason, Pandora, Hercules, Achilles and so on. Discuss their characteristics and strengths. Also talk about the types of beasts these characters have to fight, . minotaurs and so on. Model how to devise characters using a frame similar to a wanted poster that shows their strengths and characteristics. Encourage the children to be as imaginative as possible in their descriptions and names of the characters they create. **Independent work** Provide the children with a sheet similar to photocopiable page 48 'Story framework'. The children devise their own superhero and provide them with a history. **Plenary** Ask the children to share their own created characters and explain how these will be challenged in the story they are going to plan.	link to History understanding of Greek gods and their characteristics **Extend:** differentiate the frame you offer children to include their character's history, previous quests, strengths, any weaknesses, parentage and so on **Support:** provide a structured frame for describing their character

DAY 2 — Planning your own myth

Key features	Stages	Additional opportunities
Creative thinking: plan own myth using strategies modelled **Information processing:** thinking of the different elements in a myth	**Introduction** Use shared writing to devise the story of the myth. Explain that this is a quest story similar to *Jason and the Golden Fleece*. Explain that there should be three challenges that the superhero has to overcome before bringing back the prized object. Discuss what the prized object could be. It is essential, at this stage, to make clear what the prize is, where it is kept and who it is guarded by. Identify the purpose of the quest. Who has told the superhero to go and get the prize? Which god? What will the superhero receive as a reward? Make a link with a character created yesterday, showing how to weave some of the characteristics identified into the plot of the story. Remind the children that their planning should be only simple statements of what happens and not a whole story. **Independent work** Give the children copies of photocopiable page 48 'Story framework'. Remind them to refer to their characters devised yesterday as they plan their myth, using the strategies you have modelled. **Plenary** Invite the children to work in pairs and tell their myths to each other using their photocopiable sheets.	**Extend:** ensure children are using only one summary statement for each part of the planning process **Support:** provide children with a first challenge on the photocopiable. The children then complete the remaining tasks the hero has to face

DAY 3 ■ Writing a myth

Key features	Stages	Additional opportunities
Creative thinking: to write applying own knowledge of structures and language features of myths	**Introduction** Use shared writing to model the start of the myth. Ensure that you provide the context for the myth you are modelling, for example which god has commanded that the prize be found. Refer back to photocopiable page 48 completed in the whole-class work yesterday and also to the list of good story-telling phrases collected on Phase 3, Day 3. Use these in the writing. As you model, show the effects of direct and reported speech, and direct the children's attention to the language features you are using, for example punctuation on the run, subtle connectives and characterisation. Model only the first two paragraphs, that is the first two blocks on the photocopiable sheet. **Independent work** Using their plans from yesterday, ask the children to write their own myths. They should consider which paragraphs require more detail than others. Remind them to apply techniques such as spelling rules, punctuation conventions and dialogue layout. Make it clear that you only want them to write up to the end of the second challenge.	**Extend:** ensure the application of paragraphs and remind them of tips for good openings from Narrative Unit 1
Evaluation: evaluation of own work	**Plenary** Invite the children to select what they consider to be the most effective part of their writing and read it out loud. Ask why they chose it and what good writing tricks have been used. If appropriate, refer the children back to their own personal writing targets.	**Support:** focus on writing one clear well sequenced paragraph independently

DAY 4 ■ Using word order and connectives to improve writing

Key features	Stages	Additional opportunities
	Introduction Revise the rules for adding less common prefixes and suffixes and the rules for adding suffixes. Use the interactive activity 'Match it' from the CD-ROM to model how to create words. Choose an example of a child's writing to discuss in class. Look at the order of the events. Identify with the children where more description and events could have been added to maintain the reader's interest. Re-draft the paragraph, showing the children how to start sentences in different ways, for example not always starting with *Then he* but using different connectives.	**Extend:** correct spellings using a dictionary and use a thesaurus for more descriptive language
Evaluation: to reflect critically on own writing to edit and improve it	**Independent work** Ask the children to select their own paragraph to work on. They should read this to a response partner who can identify what they would like to know more about in the story. The children should then use these responses and teacher marking to redraft their paragraph. **Plenary** Invite the children to read out their revised paragraphs to their response partners and discuss how the changes have enhanced the writing.	**Support:** provide editing criteria, for example change phrases; include adverbs; check punctuation of simple sentences

DAY 5 ■ Completing the myth

Key features	Stages	Additional opportunities
Creative thinking: to write applying own knowledge of structures and language features of myths	**Introduction** Return the class to the modelled plan you made for the story and remind the children that the third challenge is the climax of the story as this is the one that enables the hero to go through to collect the prize and return victorious. Discuss with the children how to end the story you have devised together. Use shared writing to write the climax and ending of the story, applying the techniques taught over the course of the Unit, for example use of good story-telling phrases, description, strong authorial voice. As you write, challenge the children to identify the key language features you are using, for example direct and reported speech, story-telling connectives and descriptive words and phrases.	**Extend:** children identify any incorrect spellings in their work, ask them to create tips to remember the correct spellings
	Independent work Ask the children continue to write their own version of their myth using the characters they have planned and their list of useful words and phrases. Ensure that all children have written a completed myth by the end of this session.	
Evaluation: evaluation of own work	**Plenary** Choose some of the children to read the climax and endings to their myths. Ask these children to then re-read their whole story and identify which part they think is the most effectively written. Which techniques have they used that they are most proud of?	**Support:** provide a simple writing frame for the climax and conclusion

Guided reading
Read a range of myths from different cultures and traditions and other texts. See the web link from the CD-ROM. As children become more familiar with different myths, make connections between characters and their characteristics.

Assessment
Use the assessment sheet on the CD-ROM 'The quest for Golden Owl's Claw', to identify and analyse children's progress in this genre. Refer back to the learning outcomes on page 31.

Further work
Link to History work on The Greeks. The children choose an excerpt of their myth to publish and complete it with an illustration of a key moment in the text.

Bones of the story

Pandora's box

◼ Cut out the story and put it in the correct order.

✂ -

Pandora tried to forget about the box but she couldn't.
Zeus was angry, fire was only meant for the gods.
Epimetheus created a beautiful world filling it with living creatures. His brother created man but spent so long doing it that all the gifts had been used on the other creatures.
She opens the box and lets out Hope in the world.
Pandora opened the box and all evil, hate, despair and jealousy enter the world.
Pandora hopes Epimetheus will forgive her.
Zeus creates woman, Pandora. All the gods bestow gifts upon her.
Prometheus tried to warn Epimetheus that this was a trick. But Epimetheus fell in love with her and they were married.
Pandora hears the voice in the box again, but does not want to be tricked again.
Prometheus decides to give humans fire from the Sun.
They were given a wedding gift, a box, which must never, ever be opened.

Bones of the story

Garden of Eden

■ Cut out the story and put it in the correct order.

✂ --

Eve and Adam left the garden never to return. Anger, hate and jealousy remain in the world alongside goodness, love and hope.
The snake persuaded Eve to taste the apple on the tree asking her what possible harm it could do and why would God want to stop her eating it.
God called the garden 'Eden' and told them that they could touch and use everything in the garden except the Tree of life. He asked them not to touch it and definitely not to eat the apples that were the fruit of the tree.
Eve and Adam lived happily together in the garden but Eve was curious about the tree.
One day Eve went to the tree and stood looking at the beautiful apples. A snake came along and talked to her.
Man, named Adam, was lonely so God created Eve, a woman, out of Adam's seventh rib. They lived together in the garden.
Eve tasted the apple and immediately shame, deceit, anger and hate enter her head.
Adam challenged her asking whether she had touched or eaten the apple. Eve lied to him denying it.
God created the world in seven days and created a beautiful garden. He made man to live in the beautiful garden alongside all of the animals. All was perfect.
God is angry with them both and banishes them from the Garden of Eden saying that they can never enter in to it again as they disobeyed him and let anger, hate, lies, and fear into the world.
Later Eve admitted she had tasted the apple and persuades Adam to taste it too. He does and soon they are blaming each other for what has happened.

Creation stories

◼ Compare these two stories in the chart below.

	Pandora's Box	Garden of Eden
The setting and characters What role do the men have in the story? What are the girls like in each story?		
The temptation What makes them want to open the box or taste the apple?		
How did Pandora come to be with Epimetheus and how did Eve come to be in the Garden?		
The consequences of eating the apple and opening the box What happens to the world when the box is opened or when the apple is eaten?		

◼ 100 LITERACY FRAMEWORK LESSONS YEAR 5

PHOTOCOPIABLE ▪SCHOLASTIC
www.scholastic.co.uk

Pandora's justification

'I did it because .....'

★ Main reason

★ Elaboration

★ A second reason

★ Elaboration

★ A third reason

★ Elaboration

Name _____ Date _____

Story framework

Who is my hero?
_____

Which god has commanded this quest?
_____

Who does your hero have to get past to get the reward?
_____

Three challenges the hero must face

1. _____

2. _____

3. _____

The object or power my hero brings back
_____

The challenge is set

The hero's first challenge

The hero's second challenge

The hero's third challenge

What my hero gets at the end and what he takes back

NARRATIVE
UNIT 3 Stories from other cultures

Speak and listen for a range of purposes on paper and on screen

Strand 4 Drama
- Reflect on how working in role helps explore complex issues.

Read for a range of purposes on paper and on screen

Strand 6 Word structure and spelling.
- Group and classify words according to their spelling patterns and meanings.

Strand 7 Understanding and interpreting texts
- Infer writer's perspectives from what is written and what is implied.
- Compare different types of narrative and information texts and identify how they are structured.

Strand 8 Engaging with and responding to texts
- Reflect on reading habits and preferences and plan personal reading goals.

Write for a range of purposes on paper and on screen

Strand 9 Creating and shaping texts
- Reflect independently and critically on own writing and edit and improve it.
- Experiment with different narrative forms and styles to write own stories.
- Vary pace and develop viewpoint though the use of direct and reported speech, portrayal of action, selection of detail.

Strand 10 Text structure and organisation
- Experiment with the order of sections and paragraphs to achieve different effects.

Strand 11 Sentence structure and punctuation
- Adapt sentence construction to different text types and purposes and readers.
- Punctuate sentences accurately including the use of speech marks and apostrophes.

Progression in narrative

In this year, children are moving towards:
- Using improvisation and role play to explore different characters' points of view; retelling a familiar story from the point of view of another character, using spoken language imaginatively to entertain the listener.
- Planning and rewriting a familiar story from an alternative point of view; trying to vary pace by using direct and reported speech; varying sentence length and include examples of complex sentences; using a range of connectives effectively to create links and indicate changes in time or place.

▶

UNIT 3 ◄ Stories from other cultures continued

Key aspects of learning covered in this Unit

Evaluation
As they read and compare the work of particular authors, children will express and justify their judgements about books and about the author's style.

Enquiry
Children will decide how to answer questions about an author by using different sources of information, surveys of opinion and so on.

Creative thinking
Children will work in role, developing ideas to deepen understanding of the text with which they are working.

Social skills
Children will participate in an extended group activity. They will take on a clearly defined role in the group, negotiate with others and reach agreement.

Self-awareness
Children will discuss and reflect on their personal responses to the texts.

Communication
Children will develop their ability to discuss as they work collaboratively in paired, group and whole-class contexts. They will communicate outcomes orally, in writing and through ICT if appropriate.

Prior learning

Before starting this Unit check that the children can:
■ Plan, tell and write complete stories with a clear sequence of events and showing how one event leads to another; use detailed description and powerful verbs to evoke setting and portray characters.
■ Participate in group discussion by offering reasons for their opinions supported by evidence, summarising ideas, reaching agreement and presenting ideas to an audience.
■ Talk about books by a favourite author, explaining why they enjoy them and how and why the books were written.
If they need further support please refer to a prior Unit or a similar Unit in Year 4.

Resources

Recommended class novel: *The Baboons Who Went This Way and That* by Alexander McCall Smith; *Spider's web* from *Tales from Africa*, retold by Kathleen Arnott ✿; *Bre-nancy and the 13 Plantains Extracts 1* and *2* from *Stories from the Caribbean* by Petronella Breinburg ✿; *Amul and the Drum* by Campbell Perry ✿; Audio file *The Sea Woman* by Campbell Perry ✿; Photocopiable page 62 'Story comparison'; Photocopiable page 63 'Writing a letter'; Photocopiable page 64 'Character comparison'; Photocopiable page 65 'Story structure'; Photocopiable page 66 'Interviewing characters'; Assessment activity 'Match the genre' ✿

Cross-curricular opportunities

Geography
History

UNIT 3 ■ Teaching sequence

Phase	Children's objectives	Summary of activities	Learning outcomes
1	I can infer writers' perspectives from what is written and what is implied. I can identify use of language to create particular effects in narrative. I can reflect on how working in role helps explore complex issues. I can reflect on reading habits and explore preferences	Read CD-ROM *Spider's web* to identify key words and phrases to show characteristics and the authorial voice. Use CD-ROM extracts *Spider's web* and *Bre-nancy and the 13 Plantains* to identify language effects. Interview characters from *Spider's web* to identify alternative point of view. Write letters from characters' point of view. Compare characters in stories using photocopiable page 64.	Children can highlight texts showing phrases that indicate character and authorial voice. Children can identify and explain key phrases. Children can work in role and empathise with characters. Children can highlight similarities and differences between characters.
2	I can revise the punctuation of dialogue to convey an action, and add detail. I can compare oral and written versions . I can identify and apply authorial voice to narrative storytelling and writing. I can understand the use of direct and reported speech.	Revise rules of punctuation of dialogue. Children improvise conversations between characters. Use *The Sea Woman* (audio on CD-ROM). Analyse oral and written storytelling. Use photocopiable page 65. Children write own versions of *The Sea Woman* in the first person. Use CD-ROM extract *Spider's web* to identify direct and reported speech.	Children can improvise scenes. Children can complete statements that tell the end of a story. Children can write a version of a story from another character's point of view told in the first person. Children can understand and use direct and reported speech.
3	I can experiment with narrative form to write own stories. I can adapt sentence structure to different text types and readers. I can use role play to reflect on character's choices and motivations. I can plan own story based on a story from another culture. I can orally retell it from alternative point of view. I can write own version from different character's perspective. I can experiment with the order of sections and paragraphs to achieve effects. I can revise and edit own writing to achieve final version.	Use CD-ROM extract *Bre-nancy and the 13 Plantains* to discuss moral messages. Children write an alternative ending. Children identify a number of text types. Children write own versions of a sentence in different text types. Interview and compare characters from the CD-ROM extracts. Children then write in role as one of them. Use photocopiable page 65 to plan own story. Children retell their story orally. Children write own versions of the story from an alternative point of view in both third person and first person. Children revise one paragraph identifying areas to add more detail and reorder the sentences. Children revise part of their story and create own sound/audio file .	Children can write own ending to a story showing moral message. Children can write the same sentence in different text forms with changes to the structure identified. Children can write in role as one of the characters. Children can write an original story planned using the story planner. Children can write first part of own story applying authorial voice and direct and reported speech. Children can take part in paired discussion and revision of one paragraph exploring the effects of reordering. Children can create an audio file of their story.

Provide copies of the objectives for the children.

DAY 1 ■ Spider's web

Key features	Stages	Additional opportunities
Enquiry: infer writer's perspectives from what is written and what is implied	**Introduction** Explain to the children that the Unit is going to look at stories from different cultures and countries. Most of these stories have been told over the generations and passed down. Explain that some of the stories will be similar to traditional tales. Outline to the children the different aspects of the Unit and the work they will be doing, for example looking at dialogue, writing from different points of view and writing their own story. Introduce the story *Spider's web* from the CD-ROM. Explain the events prior to the story: *The animals are lonely, wondering how they can find wives. Hare tells them he knows that there are plenty of wives up in the sky beyond the clouds and Spider suggest he spins a web ladder to climb up there.* Read the extract with the children, identifying the narrative voice by text marking on screen, for example *Not so hare, Of course, Even hare was surprised.* Discuss how these different phrases indicate the storyteller has an opinion of the characters' behaviour. Deduce with the children from these phrases and others what that opinion might be.	**Extend:** provide children with more areas to identify within the text including narrative voice, characters' behaviour and so on
	Independent work Give pairs of children copies of the extract and ask them to identify where the narrative voice occurs, key connectives in the storytelling, phrases and words that identify the character of the hare and the spider.	**Support:** provide specific items to scan for in the text, such as names, phrases that the children can then explain
	Plenary Discuss the phrases and words children select and discuss by returning to the text. Record the phrases and words on a whiteboard or flipchart.	

DAY 2 ■ Spider's web – use of language

Key features	Stages	Additional opportunities
Enquiry: identify use of language to create particular effects in narrative	**Introduction** Return to *Spider's web.* Identify with the children the differing techniques used by the author to tell the story effectively, for example use of narrative voice, contrasting characters, use of direct speech to show characters, and reported speech to keep the narrative moving. Record examples of these and their effects on a chart on the board. Discuss with the children how these devices are effective, for example they keep the pace going. Repeat this with Extract 1 and 2 *Bre-nancy and the 13 Plantains* from the CD-ROM. Discuss with the children the style in which the different stories are told.	
	Independent work Provide the children with copies of *Spider's web* or *Amul and the drum* from the CD-ROM. Ask them to identify key words and phrases they think are effective. They should also identify key narrative techniques that have been used, such as narrative voice, types of connectives, characterisation, structure. Use photocopiable page 62 'Story comparison' to support the children in this activity. Remind them to explain the images and the effect of the phrases upon the reader.	**Extend:** children explain in their own words narrative devices that were effective **Support:** spend extra time reading *Amul and the drum* with the children for extra support
	Plenary Create a list entitled *Narrative devices* on a board or flipchart. Record the examples the children give from the texts they have studied and discuss.	

DAY 3 ■ Looking closely at characters

Key features	Stages	Additional opportunities
	### Introduction Recap with the children Spider's and Hare's actions in *Spider's web*. Discuss with the children the way hares act in other stories they know, for example the fable *The Hare and the Tortoise*. Discuss the characteristics of hares and why in story tradition they may be labelled as cunning (for example, their speed means they can get away with much more than other animals).	
Creative thinking: reflect on how working in role helps explore complex issues	### Speaking and listening In pairs, ask the children to think of questions they would like to ask Hare about his actions. Explain to the children that they are going to use a technique called hot-seating to interview Hare. Choose one child to take the role of Hare while the others question the character. Repeat this with other children taking on the role of Hare, encouraging them to provide different reasons for their actions. Model briefly for the children a letter from Hare to Spider defending his actions and trickery. Show the children how to expand on their reasons by adding extra details. A starting sentence could be: *It wasn't really my fault...*	**Extend:** encourage the children to write as much detail in their letters as possible
	### Independent work The children write their own letter expressing the reasons why Hare did what he did in the story. Encourage them to use their insights from the hot-seating activity to enhance their writing.	**Support:** provide a simple writing frame to help structure their letters
	### Plenary Read examples from the children's letters to the class. Ask the children to identify whether they have expanded on the reasons for Hare's actions.	

DAY 4 ■ How are the characters different?

Key features	Stages	Additional opportunities
	### Introduction Re-read *Spider's web* and Extracts 1 and 2 *Bre-nancy and the 13 Plantains* from the CD-ROM. Create a chart for comparing the main characters on a board or flipchart. Identify phrases and events that differ between the two stories. Record them under the following headings: actions/behaviour of characters, main events, resolution, narrative techniques used. Identify the different elements by highlighting on the extracts and then recording these on the chart and adding your own notes.	**Extend:** the children search and collect different books containing traditional tales or stories from different cultures and display in the book corner
Evaluation: reflect on reading habits and explore preferences	### Independent work Provide the children with photocopiable page 64 'Character comparison' and copies of either *Spider's web*, *Bre-nancy and the 13 Plantains* or *Amul and the drum* (differentiated text). The children record the similarities and differences between the characters on the grid.	**Support:** simplify the photocopiable sheet for children who are struggling to compare the stories
	### Plenary Discuss the characters in each story and the children's preferences.	

Guided reading

Read a range of stories from other cultures and traditions to discuss narrative devices and storytelling techniques.

Ensure that discussions take place where children are encouraged to deduce and infer, explaining their reasoning orally.

Assessment

Informally assess children's ability to make simple inferences about what is implied in the text and the word choices the author uses through whole-class work, guided work and marking.

Refer back to the learning outcomes on page 51.

Further work

Encourage parents to come in and tell stories from their culture or tradition so that children hear a variety of different audio styles. Discuss similarities and differences between the stories told.

Use the internet to research other stories from different cultures

Invite storytelling groups into school to work with children.

Read as a class novel *The Baboons Who Went This Way and That* by Alexander McCall Smith.

DAY 1 ◼ How do I punctuate direct speech?

Key features	Stages	Additional opportunities
	Introduction Use *Spider's web* and focus closely on the dialogue within the extract. Discuss with children the following aspects and rules of dialogue: ■ Reporting clauses developed into actions using the word 'as', for example *'What are you talking about?' asked Spider, as the other animals crowded round him.* ■ Adverbs used more sparingly to achieve effects and not used in every reporting clause. ■ Sentences can be punctuated within speech marks.	
Creative thinking: use role play to understand and revise dialogue	**Speaking and listening** In threes, ask the children to act out the scene from the extract up until Hare accuses Spider. Discuss the actions of the characters. Choose a few groups to act out their role plays for the class. Select one of these role plays to use as a model for writing a dialogue. Scribe it with the children, discussing how to add a clause starting with 'as' into the reporting clause and how to use adverbs to enhance the writing.	**Extend:** include an action starting with 'as' in more than one clause of direct speech
	Independent work Invite the children to write their own conversations from the role plays they have carried out.	**Support:** focus on securing the correct punctuation of direct speech
	Plenary Recap the key aspects of writing dialogue and dialogue punctuation. Choose some of the children to read out their written conversations to the class and discuss them.	

DAY 2 ◼ Oral stories

Key features	Stages	Additional opportunities
Evaluation: compare oral and written versions of stories	**Introduction** As a class, discuss the differences between oral stories and written stories and the effects upon the reader and listener. Use the audio version of *The Sea Woman* from the CD-ROM. Ask the children to listen to the different techniques that have been used in this oral story. Record their comments on a board.	
	Speaking and listening Use photocopiable page 65 'Story structure' to put together the events in *The Sea Woman*. Organise the class into a circle and provide a storytelling conch (any nice 'touchy feely' object to pass round the circle). Explain that the person with the conch is the one who has the chance to speak. When they have finished, they pass the conch on. Using this technique, retell *The Sea Woman*. Discuss with the children the storytelling techniques they have used. Include gesture and different vocal expressions.	**Extend:** the children orally explain why they think their new ending is effective
Creative thinking: write own ending to an oral story	**Independent work** Using the photocopiable page ask the children to create their own endings to *The Sea Woman* story by writing notes to remind them of events.	**Support:** encourage speaking in more than one sentence when they take part in the storytelling activity
	Plenary Gather the children in a circle again and invite the children to tell their endings to *The Sea Woman*. Identify the storytelling techniques used.	

DAY 3 ■ Oral retelling

Key features	Stages	Additional opportunities
Creative thinking: identify and apply authorial voice to narrative story telling and writing	**Introduction** Recap with the children what they did yesterday to add their own ending to *The Sea Woman*. Draw up a list of different storytelling techniques. Explain that they are going to retell *The Sea Woman* from the point of view of the seal woman. What would be the important things in the story that she would want to tell? For example, when the fisherman trapped her and took her to his home; how this made her feel; her marriage to the fisherman and the birth of her daughter; her escape. Show the children how to change the events noted on photocopiable page 65 to show the story from the perspective of the seal woman (remind them of the use of the first person). **Speaking and listening** Provide the children with their own copy of photocopiable page 65. In pairs, ask the children to plan a retelling of the story from the seal woman's point of view, using notes only. The children should assess each others' oral retelling against a checklist of storytelling techniques that you have drawn up, for example change of voice for different characters, use of gesture, eye contact, simple sound effects. **Plenary** Choose a few children to talk about their plan of the retelling of *The Sea Woman*. Does their plan cover all elements described in the checklist? Lead a discussion about the importance of performing the story to engage the interest of the listener in the same way as you engage the reader. Encourage the children to have another go and make improvements.	**Extend:** use the first person to plan their completion of the story **Support:** recap on the difference between first and third person in text

DAY 4 ■ Direct and reported speech

Key features	Stages	Additional opportunities
Evaluation: understand the difference between direct and reported speech and apply in writing	**Introduction** Return to *Spider's web* and focus on the part of the text starting with the phrase, *Of course all the animals protested.* Identify the examples of direct speech by highlighting the extract. Highlight: *All the animals protested; the woman agreed* and discuss with the children how these comments from characters would be written if they were in direct speech. Record their ideas on the board. **Independent work** Provide the children with examples of direct speech that you have either made up yourself or from other texts. Tell the children to turn these into reported speech and highlight the words that are different. **Plenary** Return to *Spider's web* and discuss with the children how the direct and reported speech is balanced so as not to take up the whole story with conversation. Then discuss the examples of reported speech that the children have produced from the independent work. Point out that reported speech is also a device for moving the story on.	**Extend:** children write their own direct speech and change it to reported speech **Support:** secure the use of punctuation of direct speech

Guided reading

Maintain children's interest in the genre by focusing on the plot sequences in the different stories that they are reading. Identify similarities and differences between the characters.

Assessment

Informally identify children who have difficulty talking for extended periods of time. Make informal analysis of whether they have problems with sequencing ideas, range of vocabulary, accurate precise nouns and so on. For EAL learners, observe and record whether they omit articles in their speech or whether they muddle tenses in their storytelling. From this, teach as necessary.

Refer back to the learning outcomes on page 51.

Further work

Encourage parents to come in and tell stories to the children using some of the techniques identified in the teaching.

DAY 1 ▪ A new ending

Key features	Stages	Additional opportunities
Enquiry: to experiment with narrative forms to write own stories and apply what they know about direct and reported speech	**Introduction** Use Extracts 1 and 2 *Bre-nancy and the 13 Plantains* from the CD-ROM to remind the children of the plot. Recap on the characters' motives in the story and how the story ends. Discuss the ending with the children and what its key message is. Discuss what other moral messages could be told through a story. How could the story end and give the reader a different message? What else would need to change? What events and actions would need to be added to make the new ending work? Record children's ideas on the board or flipchart, making explicit the connection between the moral and the action/event, for example in *Bre-nancy* the moral is not to be greedy shown by Bre-nancy tricking his children into giving him their plantains. **Speaking and listening** Use paired talk to discuss the possible actions that Bre-nancy could take at the end of the story to give a different moral message. Record the children's ideas on a board, for example Bre-nancy might decide not to eat all the plantains but give some away and so on. **Independent work** Using shared writing, model for the children how an alternative ending could be written that shows a different moral. Demonstrate how to incorporate direct and reported speech. The children should then choose a different moral and the actions and events that illustrate it from those recorded on the board and write their own ending. **Plenary** Invite the children to read their endings, discussing how the moral is illustrated.	if timing allows, revise strategies to spell words with common spelling patterns, for example doubling and homophones **Extend:** write two alternate endings with different morals **Support:** work in a small group to write the alternative ending together prior to their independent writing

DAY 2 ▪ Which text type is it?

Key features	Stages	Additional opportunities
Enquiry: adapt sentence structure to different text types	**Introduction** On a flipchart or board provide the children with examples of sentences from different text types, such as recount, information text, story, report. As you do so, discuss the different language features and sentence constructions (for example, present tense) used. **Independent work** Provide children with two different sentences, for example: *To play a football match you need to have the following:* *Charlton football club plays in the premier league.* Ask the children to create sentences about the same subject as if they came from the following kinds of text: instructions, report, recount, suspense narrative, traditional tale and so on. **Plenary** Take feedback from the sentences and discuss changes to the sentence construction and language features.	**Extend:** children create their own sentences of different text types around a common theme or idea **Support:** provide different sentences of different text types and ask the children to match them to the text type

DAY 3 Characters' behaviour

Key features	Stages	Additional opportunities
	### Introduction	
	Remind the children of three different characters that have appeared in the CD-ROM resources: Hare (*Spider's web*); Bre-nancy (*Bre-nancy and the 13 Plantains*) and the fisherman (*The Sea Woman*). Explain to the children that they are going to interview all of them to find out why they behaved in the way they did in the stories. This is also an opportunity to make explicit some of the similarities between the stories, for example they contain items that are local to the area or native to the country, such as plantains, seals.	bring plantains into school so children are familiar with them
Creative thinking: use role play to reflect on character's choices and motivations	### Speaking and listening	
	In pairs, tell the children to think of their questions and record these on their individual whiteboards. They could also use photocopiable page 66 'Interviewing characters'. Remind them to focus their questions on the actions and behaviour of the characters. Conduct interviews with the three characters before the whole class.	**Extend:** write a short paragraph from the perspective of each of the three characters interviewed
	### Independent work	
	Tell the children to choose a character to write in role, explaining why they had to do what they did, for example why the fisherman trapped the seal woman and hid her seal skin; why Bre-nancy wanted the plantain and so on. Explain to the children that they could write in a letter or diary form.	
	### Plenary	**Support:** provide and plan questions that they would like to ask
	Discuss with the children why these stories might have been told, for example to teach a moral message. Then choose a few children to read out their diary entries or letters and discuss these as a class.	

DAY 4 Planning my own story

Key features	Stages	Additional opportunities
	### Introduction	
	Model for the children the process of planning a story using shared writing. Remind them of the different aspects of the story that link to the setting. Identify with the children an appropriate problem (again linked to the setting,) such as the character needs something such as wives or food or fuel. Use photocopiable page 65 'Story structure' to break the events of the story down into small steps. Provide the children with clear steps in the planning process to show how the problem is resolved.	
		Extend: the children write about the characteristics of their story characters
Creative thinking: plan own story based on a story from another culture	### Independent work	
	Give the children copies of the photocopiable sheet to write a plan for their own story, using the prompts on the sheet for guidance. Remind them to think carefully about how the setting and characters provide the context to solve the problem.	
	### Plenary	**Support:** provide the children with the start of a story which they have to finish
	Ask the children to show you their story planning frames and discuss these. Discuss the characters, setting, context, problem, and the ending of the story. How do the children think they can improve their planning? Does it need to be revised in anyway? Ask them to finalise their plans before moving on to writing their stories.	

DAY 5 ■ Writing a story

Key features	Stages	Additional opportunities
	## Introduction	
	Use shared writing to model the process of writing a story, applying the planning from Day 4. As you model, make explicit to the children the use of the phrases and techniques to create a strong authorial voice, for example *Now there once was... But of course the hare... It goes without saying that the hare did not think this a good idea.* Show the children also how you have applied the use of both direct and reported speech in context to make the writing balanced. As you write, ask the children to identify the techniques you have used. Discuss also how and why commas have been used in the writing to divide phrases and clauses.	**Extend:** write two paragraphs of the story in the first person and then rewrite the first paragraph in the third person to see the differences
	After modelling the story in the third person, discuss with children how the story would change when written from the perspective of the main character. Explain that this would be in the first person. Use shared writing to create a paragraph with the children from the point of view of the main character. Show them how the strong authorial voice can be maintained.	
Creative thinking: write own version of the story from different character's perspective	## Independent work	**Support:** write the end to the story in the third person, structuring events clearly, provide support as necessary
	Ask the children to write the first paragraphs of their story in the third person, and then write the opening paragraph from the point of view of one of the characters (the first person).	
	## Plenary	
	Ask some of the children to read their two contrasting paragraphs. Discuss the strength of the authorial voice in both paragraphs and the effects.	

DAY 6 ■ Paragraph order

Key features	Stages	Additional opportunities
	## Introduction	
	Use an example of one of the children's paragraphs, enlarge and display it, or photocopy it for each child. Remind the children of the purpose of this session: to reflect upon the order of items within a paragraph. Explain that it is important to identify areas where the reader might want to know more. Ask the children to read the paragraph in pairs and then discuss what they would like to know more about, for example further details of the characters' feelings and thoughts or more description about the setting.	
Evaluation: experiment with the order of sections and paragraphs to achieve effects	Model how they can reorder the sentences in the paragraph to improve the way the paragraph reads. Show the children two ways to order the paragraph to show the differences. Discuss which they think reads better and is more effective.	**Extend:** the children edit and revise the order and sentences of their paragraphs
	## Independent work	**Support:** provide the children with a set of separate sentences that, put together, form a paragraph; the children reorder them
	Ask the children to pair up and choose a paragraph of writing to improve from their own writing. They should firstly identify the things that they, as readers, want to know more about. Then they should individually rewrite the paragraph, adding in the improvements identified and rearranging the order in which things are said.	
	## Plenary	
	Ask the children to get back into their pairs and to read their paragraphs, invite them to discuss which is more effective and why.	

DAY 7 ■ Recording the story

Key features	Stages	Additional opportunities
	### Introduction Re-read with the children the story that was modelled on Day 5 and remind them about oral storytelling. Explain how to identify parts of the story that could have sound effects, change of voice, pace and rhythm. Explain to the children that in this lesson they are going to make recordings of their stories.	
Creative thinking: revise and edit own writing to achieve a final recorded version	### Independent work Tell the children to return to the stories that they have written and identify the parts in their story that they think would need sound effects, change of voice, pace and rhythm. They may at this stage want to add in extra examples of the narrative voice and make changes to particular phrases, as they may not sound effective when spoken aloud.	**Extend:** children retell their stories orally by identifying and revising the main parts
	### Speaking and listening Invite the children to rehearse their stories orally, with partners listening and providing feedback. Encourage them to refine their sound effects so that they are confident that the story is the best it can be. Then ask the children to make their own recordings, using ICT equipment or a tape recorder.	**Support:** use simple sequences to tell their story
	### Plenary As a class, listen to the children's audio files and discuss the storytelling aspects. Discuss whether there a was a clear authorial voice and if the story was told from a specific perspective.	

Guided reading

Read a range of traditional stories from other cultures to the children. Focus their attention to the following:
■ storytelling techniques
■ how the setting, problem and characters are intertwined
■ how the writer conveys a message or theme
■ the language chosen and its effects.

Assessment

Informally assess the children's writing against their personal and group targets.
Focus closely on how the children have applied the teaching of:
■ authorial voice
■ consistency of person in narrative
■ use of setting and problem linked together
■ use of commas to punctuate sentences and clauses.
Use the interactive assessment 'Match the genre' on CD-ROM.
Refer back to the learning outcomes on page 51.

Further work

The children create a full version of their story and in groups make a sound file of the storytelling it in groups. Publish it on the school website.
Invite parents from different cultural backgrounds to come and tell their stories. Children rewrite these versions or make their own audio versions.

Story comparison

■ Fill in the chart by identifying key narrative techniques used.

Comparison of Structure and Language Features of Stories		
	Spider's web	**Amul and the drum**
Phrases that convey a narrative voice Such as: *Now there once was*		
Types of connectives used to join ideas and events in the story Such as: *later on… while…*		
Summary of main events in the story		
Effective phrases identified Such as: *The sky shimmered – I like the word shimmered. It is a powerful verb.*		

PHOTOCOPIABLE

Writing a letter

Your address

_____

_____

_____

_____

Date _____

Dear _____

It really wasn't my fault _____

_____

_____

_____

_____

_____

_____

_____

_____

_____

_____

From _____

Name _____ Date _____

Character comparison

■ Record similarities and differences between characters on this chart.

Comparison of main characters in Amul and the drum, Spider's web and Bre-nancy and the 13 Plantains			
	Amul	**Hare**	**Bre-nancy**
Main characters in the story			
Characteristics Of these characters Describe and then give the evidence from the text			
Behaviour of the main characters			
How the other characters respond to the main characters Comment and then give evidence from the text			

■ 100 LITERACY FRAMEWORK LESSONS YEAR 5

PHOTOCOPIABLE  ◼SCHOLASTIC
www.scholastic.co.uk

Name _____ Date _____

Story structure

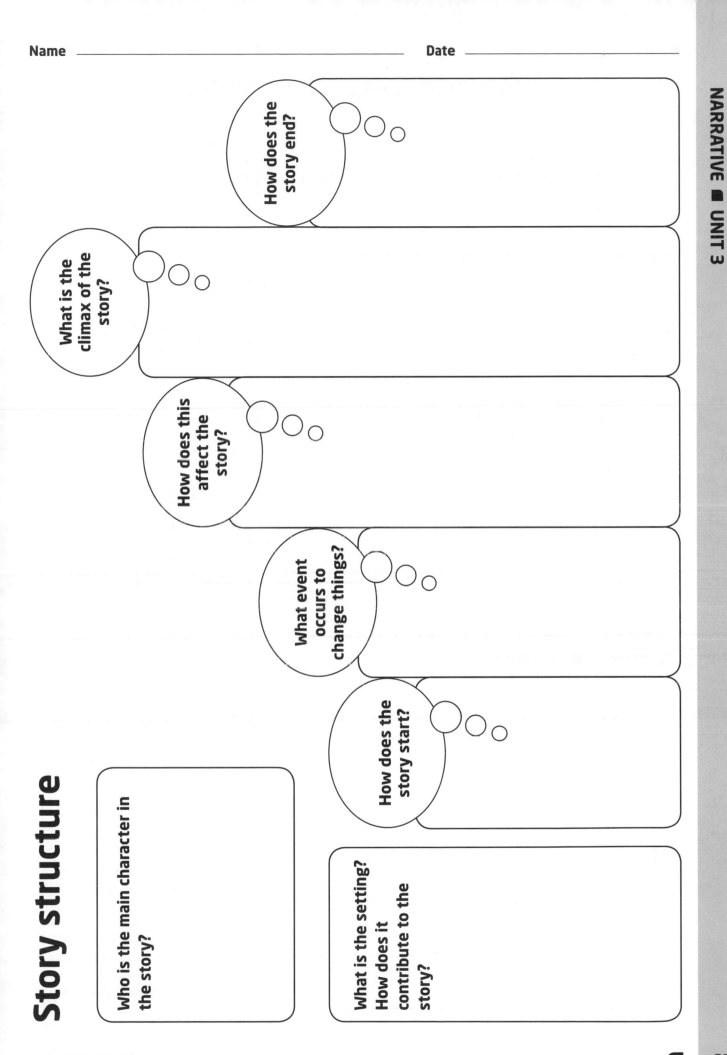

How does the story end?

What is the climax of the story?

How does this affect the story?

What event occurs to change things?

How does the story start?

Who is the main character in the story?

What is the setting? How does it contribute to the story?

Interviewing characters

■ Write down a series of open and closed questions to ask each of the characters when you interview them.

Closed question: A question that only has one answer.
For example: *Do you like the colour blue?* Yes/No

Open question: A question that has more than one answer and encourages the person to chat.

Question words: WHO? WHAT? WHERE? WHEN? WHY? HOW?

Questions for Hare

_____ | OPEN /CLOSED |

_____ | OPEN /CLOSED |

_____ | OPEN /CLOSED |

Questions for Bre-nancy

_____ | OPEN /CLOSED |

_____ | OPEN /CLOSED |

_____ | OPEN /CLOSED |

Questions for the fisherman

_____ | OPEN /CLOSED |

_____ | OPEN /CLOSED |

_____ | OPEN /CLOSED |

NARRATIVE
UNIT 4 Older literature

Speak and listen for a range of purposes on paper and on screen

Strand 2 Listening and responding
■ Identify some different aspects of talk which vary between formal and informal.

Read for a range of purposes on paper and on screen

Strand 6 Word structure and spelling
■ Know and use less common prefixes and suffixes such as -im, -ir, -cian.
Strand 7 Understanding and interpreting texts
■ Infer writers' perspectives from what is written and from what is implied.
Strand 8 Engaging with and responding to texts
■ Reflect on reading habits and preferences and plan personal reading goals.

Write for a range of purposes on paper and on screen

Strand 9 Creating and shaping texts
■ Reflect independently and critically on own writing and edit and improve it.
■ Adapt non-narrative forms and styles to write fiction or factual texts.
■ Vary pace and develop viewpoint through the use of direct and reported speech, portrayal of action and selection of detail.
Strand 10 Text structure and organisation
■ Experiment with the order of sections and paragraphs to achieve different effects.
Strand 11 Sentence structure and punctuation
■ Punctuate sentences accurately including the use of speech marks and apostrophes.

Progression in narrative

In this year, children are moving towards:
■ Considering the time and place where a 'classic' story is set and looking for evidence of differences that will affect the way that characters behave or the plot unfolds.
■ Looking at characters' appearance, actions and relationships in older literature and making deductions about differences in patterns of relationships and attitudes in comparison to children's own experience.
■ Looking at examples of dialogue and degrees of formality and considering what this shows about relationships.
■ Writing in the style of a particular author to complete a section of a story, adding dialogue or a new chapter.

Key aspects of learning covered in this Unit

Evaluation
As they read and compare the work of particular authors, children will express and justify their judgments about books and about the author's style.

Enquiry
Children will decide how to answer questions about an author by using different sources of information, surveys of opinion, and so on.

Social skills
Children will participate in an extended group activity. They will take on a clearly defined role in the group, negotiate with others and reach agreement.

Self-awareness
Children will discuss and reflect on their personal responses to the texts.

Communication
Children will develop their ability to discuss as they work collaboratively in paired, group and whole-class contexts. They will communicate outcomes orally, in writing and through ICT if appropriate.

Prior learning

Before starting this Unit check that the children can:
■ Discuss and comment on the features of narrative writing identifying key themes, characters and ideas.
■ Are able to identify techniques the author uses to keep the reader's interest.
■ Write short pieces of narrative text in different genres.
If they need further support please refer to a prior Unit or a similar Unit in Year 4.

Resources

Recommended Class Novel: *The Ghost of Thomas Kempe* by Penelope Lively; *The Ghost of Thomas Kempe Extracts 1, 2, 3, 4* and *5* ; *The Lottie Project Extracts 1* and *2* by Jacqueline Wilson ; Story mountain ; Photocopiable page 80 'Old and modern English'; Photocopiable page 81 'Story statements – *The Ghost of Thomas Kempe*'; Photocopiable page 82 'Planning a news report'; Assessment activity 'Tracking my progress in writing'

Cross-curricular opportunities

History

UNIT 4 ■ Teaching sequence

Phase	Children's objectives	Summary of activities	Learning outcomes
1	I can identify through reading how characters are introduced. I can identify aspects of talk which vary between formal and informal. I can write in role as the main character I can revise spellings of common prefixes and suffixes and revise how sentences can be extended with the use of phrases and clauses.	Use CD-ROM extract to show how the author introduces Thomas Kempe. Analyse the tricks the author uses to maintain the reader's interest. Use Extract 2 from the CD-ROM to collect evidence of the difference between the times that each character is in. Children interview James to find his viewpoint. Write a journal entry of James' thoughts and feelings. Practise spelling of prefixes and suffixes by identifying different aspects of words. Develop and expand sentences by revising how to add phrases, relative clauses and subordinate clauses.	Children can understand how characters are introduced. Children can use a comparison grid between times completed. Children can write a journal entry in role as James. Children can write sentences showing strategies for improvements by adding clauses.
2	I can identify structure of the story and key moments. I can infer writer's perspectives from what is written and what is hinted at. I can vary pace and develop viewpoint through the use of direct and reported speech in writing. I can analyse the effect of language.	Use photocopiable page 81 to help structure the main events and high and low points of the story. They write this in their journals. The children role play a scene from *Thomas Kempe*. The children write their own version of the scene in Extract 3 from the point of view of Thomas Kempe. Use Extract 5 from CD-ROM for focusing on direct and reported speech. Write a journal entry in James' diary, using direct and reported speech. Use Extract 4 from the CD-ROM to analyse the language features and vocabulary.	Children can write about story structure and write a journal extract. Children can apply skills of direct and reported speech in writing. Children can write James' journal entry of the discussion of the exorcism. Children can text mark extracts identifying language effects and explaining them.
3	I can collect and identify features of the author's style. I can to use non-narrative forms to write fiction or factual texts. I can plan and use non-narrative forms to write fiction or factual texts. I can use non-narrative forms to write fiction or factual texts. I can plan and role play in the style of the author. I can write in the style of the author. I can critically reflect on writing to edit and improve it.	Recap on extracts read and identify aspects of the author's style. Children role play characters from *The Ghost of Thomas Kempe*. They make notes using photocopiable page 82 to plan a newspaper article. Children are newspaper reporters collating evidence for writing a story. They plan a newspaper report for the local paper. The children write their own newspaper report, applying their understanding of direct and reported speech. Children role play a new scene between Kempe and James. Children write a new scene in a similar style to that of the author. The children independently improve a paragraph of their new scenes.	Children can write a scene similar to an author's style. Children can use notes collected from the interviews conducted in role play. Children can plan newspaper report for local paper. Children can draft newspaper report for local paper. Children can produce an oral outcome of a scene. Children can write new scenes in the style of the author. Children can improve their own paragraphs.

Provide copies of the objectives for the children.

DAY 1 ■ The Ghost of Thomas Kempe

Key features	Stages	Additional opportunities
Evaluation: identify through reading how characters are introduced	**Introduction** If possible, read *The Ghost of Thomas Kempe* as a class novel so that children are familiar with the story and what has happened prior to starting this Unit. Explain to the children that this Unit is going to look closely at the novel. All the work undertaken will be around this text. Use Extract 1 from the CD-ROM to explore how the character of Thomas Kempe is introduced. Identify with the children the clues the writer gives about Kempe, for example spidery writing, use of language such as *I lyke not this quille*. Discuss with the children how the author keeps the interest of the reader. **Independent work** Provide the children with copies of Extract 1. Ask them to track James' thoughts as he gradually works out that the red writing must be something sinister. **Plenary** Take feedback from the children about their deductions. Create a chart on the board that records the children's deductions and reference these to phrases in the text.	discuss different uses of language, for example, old English and modern English **Extend:** children create a grid to record phrases they have identified **Support:** provide a sheet with key questions about the text to answer

DAY 2 ■ Old and modern English

Key features	Stages	Additional opportunities
Evaluation: identify aspects of talk which vary between formal and informal	**Introduction** Read *The Ghost of Thomas Kempe Extract 2* with the children, reminding them where it comes from in the story (when James is beginning to suspect that there might really be a ghost). Discuss the evidence in the text that suggests Thomas Kempe comes from a different time. Identify and explain the following words: *alchemie, astronomie, physicke*. Explain some of the historical references, for example that in Thomas Kempe's time astronomie was the study of stars because they were still discovering where the world was in relation to the sun. Discuss also how the spelling of words in that time were different to how they are now. **Independent work** Provide children with phrases written by Thomas Kempe from Extracts 1 and 2 and ask them to write the modern equivalents of these versions, for example *For the discoverie of goods lost* could be replaced with *Lost items can be found* or *Seek me at my dwelling which lyes at the extremitie of the East Ende Lane* could be replaced with *I live at the far end of East End Lane*. Discuss with the children the changes to the language, the types of words used and so on. Give the children photocopiable page 80 'Old and modern English' to complete the task. **Plenary** Compare the phrases used by Thomas Kempe and the modern versions. Focus on how the construction of the sentences has changed. Discuss why the language might have changed over the centuries.	show children how to deduce the meanings of words through root words, prefixes and suffixes **Extend:** provide dictionaries to look up unknown words, and etymological dictionaries for word origins **Support:** provide phrases that are easily translated

DAY 3 ■ Writing a diary extract

Key features	Stages	Additional opportunities
Self-awareness: write in role as the main character	**Introduction** Return to *The Ghost of Thomas Kempe Extracts 1* and *2* from the CD-ROM to identify with the children the thoughts and views of the main character, James, through shared reading. Highlight the evidence of James' point of view on the board. Explain that the children are going to interview James to find out more about his viewpoint (children can also draw upon their knowledge of different parts of the story from listening to the class novel).	revise the difference between open and closed questions
	Speaking and listening Use paired talk to think about the types of questions that the children would like to ask James. Choose a child to be interviewed and conduct the interviews. Model for children on the board how James' diary might begin. Use the starting sentence *I am sure there is a ghost in my room.* Remind the children that they can use the evidence from the story, and that they are writing in the first person.	**Extend:** children identify key events from the story and record them in diary form
	Independent work Tell the children to write their own versions of James' diary. Ensure that they include how James originally found out and deduced Thomas Kempe's presence. What are his feelings about it? Is he irritated by it or fearful or annoyed?	**Support:** provide a simple frame for the children to structure writing
	Plenary The children share their diary extracts and discuss them with the class.	

DAY 4 ■ Extending sentences

Key features	Stages	Additional opportunities
	Introduction Use this lesson as an opportunity to revise children's understanding of the rules for adding suffixes and prefixes. Using whiteboards, provide the children with a number of root words, for example *magic, replace, possible,* and ask them to spell the following words: *magician, impossible, irreplaceable, imperfect, imperfection,* and so on. Discuss errors made with the children and how to correct them. Show the children the following sentences: *James sat down on the bed, because his legs suddenly felt a bit odd.* *He read it through three times while Tim went to sleep in the patch of yellow sunlight from the window.* Identify with children the two main clauses in each sentence and the conjunction joining them together. Identify the phrases that have been added to provide detail.	**Extend:** provide a variety of subordinating conjunctions
Evaluation: write sentences changing structure and conjunctions	**Independent work** Ask the children to write similar sentences and to change the conjunctions. Remind them to add different phrases that add extra information to the sentences.	**Support:** provide simple conjunctions such as *but, so, if, when, as*
	Plenary Take feedback from the children on their sentences. Ask them to identify where they have added extra phrases into the sentences.	

Guided reading

Read other texts that have been written by classic authors, for example Frances Hodgson Burnett, C. S. Lewis.
Discuss the features of the plot and characters.
Identify the use of language and develop children's understanding of effects.

Assessment

Through discussion and reading, assess the children's ability to predict and discuss the text.
Refer back to the learning outcomes on page 69.

Further work

Read *The Ghost of Thomas Kempe* as a class novel to ensure that children have extended knowledge of the text and characters.
Use the internet to research the time and century that Thomas Kempe lived in.
Draw parallels with children's knowledge of Tudor times.

DAY 1 ■ The key moments of a story

Key features	Stages	Additional opportunities
Enquiry: identify the structure and key moments of a story	**Introduction** Discuss with the children their most memorable moments from different stories that they have read and use paired talk to stimulate discussion. When they identify the most exciting parts, ask them to explain why, where they were in the story and what it was in the plot that made it so exciting. Record the children's responses on a board. Explain that they are going to identify the parts of *The Ghost of Thomas Kempe* that are the most exciting. **Speaking and listening** Provide the children with copies of photocopiable page 81 'Story statements', cut up into individual strips. Ask them to arrange the statements in the order that they happen in the story and then group them into the six key events of the story, discarding those that they think are not essential to the narrative. Explain that they are going to draw their own story mountain (see the image from the CD-ROM) of the story, where the peak represents the most exciting part. Tell the children to sort the statements into order of excitement according to the story mountain. **Independent work** Ask the children to write down the reasons why they chose the particular event as the most exciting/important. Remind them that they need to explain their reasoning clearly. **Plenary** Discuss the children's reasons for the most exciting part of the story as a class.	**Extend:** provide the children with opportunities to discuss and reflect on their own reading preferences and introduce them to different authors **Support:** provide prompts and clues to help sequence the main events of the story in order

DAY 2 ■ Characters' perspectives

Key features	Stages	Additional opportunities
Evaluation: infer writer's perspectives from what is written and what is hinted at	**Introduction** Display *The Ghost of Thomas Kempe Extract 3* from the CD-ROM and ask the children to identify the evidence in the text that suggests Thomas Kempe's presence. Highlight these on the text, for example *something nudged James' foot, there was a loud crash behind him* and so on. Discuss with the children what Thomas Kempe's behaviour tells the reader about what he is thinking. Ask the children, in pairs, to find out evidence in the text that tells us what James is feeling. Record these again on the text. **Speaking and listening** The children, in pairs and through role play, interview James, explaining his version of the events in the text. **Independent work** Ask the children to write a scene by referring back to Extract 3 from the point of view of Thomas Kempe. Use the following sentence as a starting point: *Thomas Kempe stood by the mantelpiece and watched as the boy looked carefully at his letter.* **Plenary** Invite the children to read and discuss their writing and the techniques used.	**Extend:** children write their own scenes in the first person using both direct and reported speech. **Support:** children write their scenes in the third person, using direct speech

DAY 3 ■ Let's look at dialogue

Key features	Stages	Additional opportunities
	Introduction Display *The Ghost of Thomas Kempe Extract 5* from the CD-ROM to highlight, through shared reading, how the dialogue is used to show characters' perspectives and feelings, for example. *James plunged in* (use of powerful verb, showing nervousness); *He stuck it in the corner of his mouth, lit it, and said 'Just the one'* (use of action prior to speech showing calmness and confidence). Identify where the author has used direct speech and why, and where he has used reported speech. Discuss the reasons for reported speech, for example it is a technique used so not all the conversation is written down. Identify through reading how James is feeling and what he might notice about Bert's behaviour. Highlight words, actions and phrases that focus on Bert and his behaviour.	
Communication: working in role with others	**Speaking and listening** In pairs, ask the children to role play the scene between James and Bert. They then role play James telling Simon about the scene and what was said. The child in role as James should naturally use reported speech. Ensure the children discuss the scene from James' point of view and explain what he thought. Show some of these scenes to the whole class.	**Extend:** children include at least two examples of reported speech in writing
	Independent work In role, invite the children to write a diary entry as James. They should use reported speech to describe what Bert said. A suggested starting sentence could be: *I went to Bert Ellison's house today – it was odd, well, he was odd. He kept stroking his chin. I told him all about...*	**Support:** children punctuate direct speech accurately
	Plenary Invite the children to read and share their diary entries with the class.	

DAY 4 ■ Choice of words

Key features	Stages	Additional opportunities
Enquiry: analyse the effect of language in text	**Introduction** Display *The Ghost of Thomas Kempe Extract 4* from the CD-ROM and discuss, the different language features the author uses to create atmosphere and effective description. Focus on the use of precise adjectives – *leather-bound book*; powerful verbs – *blinked*; descriptive phrases – *in excitement; smack between the eyes*. Ask the children to identify where the author has used phrases that James is reading in the text, for example *weather being most agreeable, fine crop this year*. Discuss how these phrases are not what James would say.	**Extend:** give children a selection of words in order to deduce their meaning from the text
	Independent work Provide the children with copies of Extract 4 and ask them to highlight phrases that describe the room James is in and the book; unusual language that the people who wrote the diary would use; phrases that describe how James felt about the discovery.	**Support:** identify specific phrases for the children to find in the text through scanning
	Plenary Take feedback from the children. As a class discuss the parallels between the diary and James' situation.	

Guided reading

Discuss the words and phrases the author uses to create particular effects. Encourage the children to explain and explore their thoughts and ideas fully by using more than one sentence.

Assessment

Through marking of the children's writing tasks from lessons and their responses in whole class work, identify the children's ability to:

- discuss and explain imagery and language effects
- how they use direct and reported speech independently in their writing

Refer back to the learning outcomes on page 69.

Further work

Collect and classify a range of interesting words and phrases from other texts that children are reading, as well as those from *The Ghost of Thomas Kempe*. The children collate these into their own tips list/book.

DAY 1 ■ Identifying an author's style

Key features	Stages	Additional opportunities
Enquiry: to collect and identify features of the author's style	**Introduction** Use Extract 4 *The Ghost of Thomas Kempe* and an example from *The Lottie Project* from the CD-ROM to identify the differences in author style. Discuss the term *style* with the children. Explain that it is the way an author writes, how the writing sounds, the types of words and narration in the story. Show the children the extract from *The Lottie Project* and encourage them to describe how the author writes, for example first person, personal narrative, uses conversational language to gain interest of the reader, subject matter about families and feelings. Then show the children Extract 4 from *The Ghost of Thomas Kempe*. Discuss and identify the author's language and identify the style of writing, such as third person, description, objective narrative storytelling. **Independent work** Provide the children with a scene from *The Ghost of Thomas Kempe*, for example Extract 2, and ask them to write the scene using the first person/ personal narrative. **Plenary** Read the new scene written by the children. Compare this with the actual extract from Thomas Kempe. Discuss how the change in style changes the tone of the writing.	**Extend:** the children read a variety of other extracts and make notes about different author styles **Support:** provide a simple writing frame to help with scene writing

DAY 2 ■ Being a reporter

Key features	Stages	Additional opportunities
Communication: to use non-narrative forms to write fiction or factual texts	**Introduction** Explain to the children that they are going to write a newspaper report about the presence of a ghost at the house. Tell them that they are going to be reporters who are interviewing different characters from the text. Using Extract 5 *The Ghost of Thomas Kempe* (from the CD-ROM) and the children's knowledge of the story, discuss who they might interview, for example James, his mum, Bert Ellison. Tell them that their newspaper reports are going to be written over the next few days. **Speaking and listening** In pairs, ask the children to discuss the questions that they, as reporters, would want to ask, as well as the differing answers the characters might make, for example James' Mum would deny that there was any knowledge of the Ghost. Would James tell of the diary that was found and what it said? What would Bert say to the reporter about James' visit? Allow the children to refer back to the text extracts from the CD-ROM to look for evidence of how characters would behave. (They could also use their extensive knowledge of the text from reading it as a class novel if appropriate). **Independent work** Carry out the interviews, with the children being reporters. Use photocopiable page 82 'Planning a news report' as a sheet for the children to record their notes. As they carry out the interview, they should make notes on the interviewees' responses to their questions. **Plenary** Discuss with the children how they made notes, including quotes from the interviewees.	**Extend:** encourage the note making strategies, such as noting key words, writing a quote, identifying the key facts **Support:** help the children record the questions they want to ask

DAY 3 ■ Planning my scoop!

Key features	Stages	Additional opportunities
Communication: to plan and use non-narrative forms to write fiction or factual texts	**Introduction** Explain that the purpose of this lesson is to take the notes made in the lesson on Day 2 and use them to plan a newspaper report about the alleged ghost in the house. Discuss with the children some of the key features of a newspaper report, for example a leading sentence that summarises the story; evidence from people concerned; facts known about the story; direct and reported speech. Explain to the children that they need to use all the information gained from the interviews. Model for the children how to put the notes together. Ask them to identify what the key facts of the story are, for example a ghost has been reported; Bert Ellison has been round to exorcise it (he is well known in this field); strange notes in red writing have been found across the village; the diary has been found. Explain to the children that they need to decide when in the newspaper report they will reveal the facts. As a class, complete the modelled version.	use paired talk to create oral summaries for the story **Extend:** ensure as much detail as possible about the character is included
	Independent work Invite the children to map out their writing, using the notes they made on photocopiable page 82 yesterday. Remind them that they need not write in full sentences – this exercise is to collect and organise their thoughts.	**Support:** provide a set of notes, based on the role plays acted out, for the children to put together
	Plenary In pairs, invite the children to discuss headlines and leading sentences that summarise the whole story and add their own ideas to their planning sheets.	

DAY 4 ■ Writing the scoop!

Key features	Stages	Additional opportunities
	Introduction Use shared writing, to model to the children how to turn their notes into a set piece of writing for a newspaper. Make explicit how direct and reported speech can be used to good effect in newspaper reports. As you write, draw attention to the following aspects: *I need a leading sentence that summarises the story. In this first paragraph I need to write down the facts that we definitely know about the story. In this second paragraph I need to write down the views of James' mum.* Discuss the use and order of paragraphs. Encourage the children to use phrases that include facts about the character, for example *Mr Ellison, 65, of Brentwood cottages, told us that...*	
	Independent work The children should use their notes from yesterday to write their own versions. Encourage them to apply their knowledge of direct and reported speech automatically as they are writing. Remind them to read back their writing to check for sense and punctuation.	**Extend:** ensure direct and reported speech is included
Communication: work in pairs to analyse their work	**Plenary** Invite the children to read their versions with a response partner and identify how many of the key features they have got in place. Identify which key facts from the interview have been included.	**Support:** children write the interview of one character

DAY 5 ◾ A response to the report

Key features	Stages	Additional opportunities
Communication: to plan and role play in the style of the author, adding in a new chapter or scene	### Introduction Discuss with the children how Thomas Kempe would respond to the newspaper report and all the characters being interviewed. Explain to the children that they are going to imagine how he would respond when James returns to the house after the interviews have taken place. ### Speaking and listening Ask the children to imagine how Thomas would reveal himself to James. What would he do? How would James know he was there? How would Thomas react? Use Extracts 2 and 3 from the CD-ROM to remind children of the ghost's behaviour. Set the scene for the children: Thomas Kempe is going to reveal himself as a figure to James in James' room. Discuss with them how each of the two characters would react. Tell them that for this exercise Thomas Kempe is going to talk. In role, the children discuss and act out the scenario. Invite them to explore the characters' feelings by using the 'freeze-frame' technique, where the children strike a still pose and an adult asks each character to share their internal thoughts. Choose one or two examples to share with the class. Develop the children's role play by discussing the motives of the characters and how they would be feeling. Would James be curious about why Thomas haunts the house? What questions would he ask? How would Thomas respond? What kind of language would he use? ### Plenary Share a few refined scenes with the whole class. Ask the children to comment on the credibility of the characters and to suggest different ways to begin and end the scene.	create digital videos of the children's performances to discuss and use as stimuli for modelled writing on Day 6

DAY 6 ◾ A new scene

Key features	Stages	Additional opportunities
Evaluation: to identify author style	### Introduction Explain to the children that they are going to build on the scenes they developed yesterday to write a new part of the story. Recap the writing style using Extracts 1 and 3 from the CD-ROM to show how the writer conveys the difference between Thomas Kempe's character and the narrative. Using some of the children's ideas and thoughts from yesterday's freeze-frame activity, demonstrate during shared writing how the scene might be written in full prose. Use some of the following features: use of the third person; Thomas would make his presence felt by moving things before he reveals himself; the type of language he would use and so on. ### Independent work Drawing on their experience from the previous lesson, ask the children to write their own new scene between Thomas Kempe and James. Remind them that they can use dialogue, but the 'voices' of the two characters need to be very different as they come from two different centuries. ### Plenary Invite the children to share and read the best extract of their scenes.	**Extend:** encourage children to identify where their spelling errors are and what strategy they can use to correct these, such as syllabification, mnemonic, rhyme **Support:** provide a simple scaffold for writing based on a retelling of some of the scenes acted out yesterday

DAY 7 ■ Publishing the new scene

Key features	Stages	Additional opportunities
Evaluation: critically reflect on writing to edit and improve it	### Introduction Using an example of the children's writing, discuss the structure of the scene that they have written using the following questions about content and punctuation: ■ *How does the writer show what is going on in James' head? Is there enough of an insight into how he is thinking and feeling after the interviews with the press?* ■ *How has the writer made the reader aware that Thomas Kempe knows that James has spoken to the press? Does he write on a copy of James' paper, for example?* Discuss the punctuation of the piece with the children. Does it read fluently or are there sentences that need refining or improving? Choose one or two examples to show. Discuss with the children what, as the readers, they would like to know more about. Highlight these as ideas on the text. ### Independent work Provide the children with clear guidance for improving their work. Use the following as starting points to help structure the activity for them: *Read through your work and underline aspects you could say more about. Does every sentence make sense? Could you improve any?* ### Plenary Ask the children to identify their changes and improvements.	allow children to use a word processing package to write their new scene **Extend:** provide criteria for checking the writing and improving it **Support:** identify punctuation and key spelling errors

Guided reading

Continue to read classic novels by other authors. Use the opportunities to:
■ encourage children to express preferences and opinions about character and plot
■ discuss an author's particular style in conveying tension and atmosphere
■ identify how the authors use direct and reported speech in their writing.

Assessment

Informally assess the children's understanding and application of direct and reported speech through marking and responding to their work. Use the assessment task 'Tracking my progress in writing' from the CD-ROM to allow the children to make a more informal assessment of their progress, linked either to their personal targets or key objectives identified.
Refer back to the learning outcomes on page 69.

Further work

Look in more detail at newspaper reporting, both in local papers and online. Allow the children an opportunity to research what life was like in the late 1500s/1600s. Link to previous work on Henry VIII and Elizabethan times.

Old and modern English

■ Rewrite these old English phrases into the modern equivalents.

Phrase in old English	Equivalent in modern English	Words that are unfamiliar in modern English or have changed from old English
Knowe who hath stollen		
I am muche displeased for there are manie who do usurpe my worke		
Thou hast in this verie dwellynge a machine which tells if there will be muche sunshine or no		
For the discoverie of goodes loste		
Seeke me at my dwellynge which lyes at the extremitie of East Ende Lane		
I have muche skille also in such artes as alchemie, astromomie etc		
My apprentice, who dwells at the same howse		

■ 100 LITERACY FRAMEWORK LESSONS YEAR 5

PHOTOCOPIABLE

■SCHOLASTIC
www.scholastic.co.uk

Story statements – *The Ghost of Thomas Kempe*

■ Cut out the statements and use them to find the bones of the story.

✂

A police man comes to East End Cottage asking if Thomas Kempe lives there.
James Harrison and his family move into East End cottage. A room that has been shut up for years has been redecorated.
Thomas Kempe reveals himself to James via the rusty noticeboard.
James decides to try and talk to Thomas Kempe.
James talks to his friend Simon and decides to find out about ghosts at the local library.
Thomas Kempe writes on the board at school saying the James is his apprentice.
James tries to talk to his parents about ghosts and poltergeists.
James receives a strange message in red writing on a paper on top of his project book. James begins to get suspicious and tries to subtly question his family. He receives another message this time written in his mother's lipstick.
James and Bert find the grave of Thomas Kempe in the Church, open it and place the spectacles and pipe in it. A light goes out as they do it. Thomas Kempe has gone.
James finds a picture of Arnold Luckett, the man in the diary who Thomas Kempe latched on to before.
James starts getting blamed for strange things such as the prescription having different writing.
James talks to Mrs Verity and decides to find an exorcist. He visits Bert Ellison to discuss the problem.
Things get worse as Thomas Kempe starts to write on people's doors in particular Mrs Verity's and the vicar's. The local police question James. The headmaster at school discusses it with the whole school. Everything points to James.
Thomas Kempe burns down Mrs Verity's house.
Thomas Kempe shows himself to James and asks him to help him go and find his resting place. He must put in his pipe and spectacles.
Bert comes round to try again and James tells him of his discovery. They try a different way to exorsise Thomas but are interrupted.
James and Bert close the grave up and go home.
James discovers a diary in the cellar and realises Thomas Kempe has behaved like this before.
James reads the diary and finds out that Thomas Kempe was a poltergeist in the house over 100 years ago. The local vicar and the people who lived in the cottage tried to exorcise Thomas Kempe by putting him in a bottle, which was put in a crevice in the wall behind the window in James' room and plastered over. The room was shut up.
Bert Ellison comes round to East End cottage to exorcise Thomas Kempe. It doesn't work - Thomas Kempe reveals it has been tried before.

Name _____   Date _____

Planning a news report

■ Write the key points of your news report below.

Headline _____

_____

_____

Caption _____

Leading sentence/introduction (sentence summarising the story)

_____
_____
_____
_____

First interviewee (include all facts from interview including full name, age, address, occupation of the interviewee)

_____
_____
_____
_____

Second interviewee: a different point of view

_____
_____
_____
_____
_____

Third interviewee (another viewpoint adding further evidence)

_____
_____
_____
_____

100 LITERACY FRAMEWORK LESSONS YEAR 5

NARRATIVE
UNIT 5 Film Narrative

Speak and listen for a range of purposes on paper and on screen

Strand 1 Speaking
■ Tell a story using notes designed to cue techniques, such as repetition, recap and humour.
Strand 4 Drama
■ Reflect on how working in role helps to explore complex issues.

Read for a range of purposes on paper and on screen

Strand 7 Understanding and interpreting texts
■ Infer writers' perspectives from what is written and from what is implied.
■ Compare different types of narrative and information texts and identify how they are structured.
Strand 8 Engaging with and responding to texts
■ Compare the usefulness of techniques such as visualisation, prediction and empathy in exploring the meaning of texts.
■ Compare how a common theme is presented in poetry, prose and other media.

Write for a range of purposes on paper and on screen

Strand 9 Creating and shaping texts
■ Reflect independently and critically on own writing and edit and improve it.
■ Experiment with different narrative forms and styles to write their own stories.
Strand 11 Sentence structure and punctuation
■ Adapt sentence construction to different text-types, purposes and readers.
■ Punctuate sentences accurately, including use of speech marks and apostrophes.
Strand 12 Presentation
■ Use a range of ICT programs to present texts, making informed choices about which electronic tools to use for different purposes.

Progression in narrative

In this year, children are moving towards:
■ Recognising that story structure can vary in different types of story and that plots can have high and low points; noticing that the structure in extended narratives can be repeated with several episodes building up to conflict and resolution before the end of the story; analysing more complex narrative structures and narratives that do not have a simple linear chronology.
■ Knowing authors have particular styles and may have a particular audience in mind; discussing the author's perspective on events and characters; author's perspective and narrative viewpoint is not always the same – note who is telling the story, whether the author ever addresses the reader directly; checking whether the viewpoint changes at all during the story; exploring how the narration relates to events.
■ Planning and writing complete stories; organising more complex chronological narratives into several paragraph units relating to story structure; adapting for narratives that do not have linear chronology; extending ways to link paragraphs in cohesive narrative using adverbs and adverbial phrases;

▶

UNIT 5 ◄ Film Narrative *continued*

adapting writing for a particular audience; aiming for consistency in character and style.

Key aspects of learning covered in this Unit

Enquiry
Children will investigate and ask questions of film to develop their understanding. They will plan and present their own interpretations of film using different modes of communication.

Creative thinking
Children will generate and extend imaginative ideas, to respond to and interpret ideas. They will suggest hypotheses, responding imaginatively through drama and talk, making connections and understanding relationships to create a written outcome.

Information processing
Children will identify relevant information and explore patterns from a range of modes and use this to write their own versions of a visual text.

Reasoning
Children will draw inferences and make deductions to clarify, extend and follow up ideas and conclusions in their oral and written work.

Evaluation
Children will present information orally, through drama and in writing. They will make judgements and justify their views and opinions, drawing on sources to support their evaluations. Children will discuss success criteria, give feedback to others and judge the effectiveness of their own work.

Communication
Children will develop their skills to reflect critically on what they have seen. They will develop their ability to present a narrative through drama, orally and in writing, and reflect critically on their own and others' work.

Empathy
In discussing, writing and working in role, children will develop their skills to recognise and understand the perspectives of other people. They will develop their ability to identify triggers or causes of other people's emotions and actions.

Prior learning

Before starting this Unit check that the children can:
■ Identify the different contributions of music, words and images in short extracts from TV programmes or film.
■ Pose probing questions appropriate to purpose.
■ Plan, tell and write complete stories with a clear sequence of events.
■ Use paragraphs to structure a narrative.
If they need further support please refer to a prior Unit or a similar Unit in Year 4.

Resources

The Ghost of Thomas Kempe Extract 3 by Penelope Lively ✆; *The Piano* a film by Aidan Gibbons – web link ✆; Interactive activity Dartboard words ✆; Photocopiable page 95 'Comparing themes'; Photocopiable page 96 'Narrative sequence'; Photocopiable page 97 'Your character'; Photocopiable page 98 'Flashback storyboard'; Assessment activity 'Sorting and writing' ✆

Cross-curricular opportunities

History

UNIT 5 ■ Teaching sequence

Phase	Children's objectives	Summary of activities	Learning outcomes
1	I can compare the usefulness of techniques such as visualisation, prediction and empathy in exploring the meaning of texts. I can infer writer's perspectives from what is written and what is implied. I can compare how a common theme is presented in prose, poetry and other media. I can experiment with different narrative forms.	Shared viewing of *The Piano*. Children make notes in their books of initial impressions of the film. Use interactive activity 'Dartboard words' from CD-ROM. Children describe the moods of different scenes in *The Piano*. Look at different film techniques using different strategies. Complete photocopiable page 95 'Comparing themes'. Write own descriptions of specific clips from *The Piano* using different narrative techniques	Children can identify different ways to engage and interrogate text to deepen their understanding. Children can make simple inferences both orally and recorded about characters, mood and themes in film. Children can complete photocopiable sheet with aspects of film viewing identified. Children can write descriptions of particular clips in the film.
2	I can reflect on how working in role helps to explore complex issues. I can experiment with different narrative forms and styles. I can punctuate sentences accurately using speech marks. I can apply knowledge of speech marks to punctuate own writing.	Deepen children's understanding of the characters in *The Piano* through role play. Write first-person diary entries of the main character. Explore how the characters might talk to each other at different points. Write simple conversations between characters in the film and apply knowledge of speech conventions.	Children can identify background of characters. Children can write first-person diary entry of significant event in the film. Children can use and apply speech conventions. Children can write conversation between two characters.
3	I can compare different types of narrative and identify how they are structured. I can adapt sentence structure to different text types and readers. I can experiment with different narratives to write own stories. I can spell words with more complex suffixes and adapt sentence structure to different text types. I can use a range of ICT programs to present texts. I can use a range of ICT programs to present texts. I can experiment with different narrative forms and styles to write my own stories.	Discuss the narrative structure of flashback. Discuss how it is different to other narratives. Use photocopiable page 96 'Narrative sequence' Use photocopiable page 97 'Your character' to plan main character for own story. Plan own flashback narrative by drawing characters and camera angles. Improve sentences by adding phrases and clauses. Change sentences for different text types Create storyboard images using miniature people, models and use a camera to record images. Create a multimedia presentation of storyboard. Write an extract from the story board and compare with the multimedia version.	Children can identify and evaluate different narrative structures. Children can plan a character for own flashback story. Children can write a diary entry of key characters' life. Children can understand different rules for spelling words. Children can use a digital camera or web cam to photograph different scenes in story. Children can produce a multi media presentation of story. Children can write a flashback scene at key point in the story.

Provide copies of the objectives for the children.

DAY 1 ■ A film narrative

Key features	Stages	Additional opportunities
Enquiry: compare the usefulness of techniques such as visualisation, prediction and empathy in exploring the meaning of texts	**Introduction** Explain to the children that they are going to be looking at how films tell stories. Introduce the film *The Piano* using the web link from the CD-ROM to the children but try not to give them any ideas as to what it is about. Explain that they are going to watch it but at various points you are going to stop the film and ask them to record their thoughts on their individual whiteboards. Pause the film at the following points and discuss: ■ Aerial view of hands playing the piano – What might the central character be thinking about as he plays? (Empathy.) ■ When his wife kisses him on the cheek then disappears – What might have happened to his wife? (Prediction.) ■ When the little boy receives the present – Who gave him the present? Why might it be significant? (Inference/ prediction.) ■ When the boy sits next to the father and plays the piano and they smile at each other – Who is the little boy, why does the film stop there? What is left unsaid? Re-run the film again. Return to the key questions asked and discuss. **Independent work** Ask the children to record their initial thoughts about the film in their books using the following key questions: *What the film is about? What is its main theme? Why does the man play the piano alone at the start but not at the end?* **Plenary** Take feedback from the children regarding the key questions.	deepen the discussion by asking the following: *How does the film tell the story? How is this different to a written story?* **Extend:** children create a grid to record their ideas **Support:** children sequence the main events of the film in order

DAY 2 ■ How does the film maker tell us about what the characters are feeling?

Key features	Stages	Additional opportunities
Empathy: understanding the film makers perspective	**Introduction** Show the children the film again pausing at key places. Identify in each sequence how the mood changes. At each point ask the children what they can infer from the image and the music about what the characters are feeling. Lead a brief discussion about how the music helps convey the mood. **Independent work** Show the children the interactive activity 'Dartboard words' from the CD-ROM. Ask: *Which five words best describe the first scene?* Place the word that describes the mood and the scene the most effectively in the centre of the circle, the next best is placed on the second circle and so on. Other relevant words can also be placed on the outer circles if space allows, but there should only be one word in the centre. Leave the interactive activity up on the screen and show the children other scenes from *The Piano.* Ask them to write down for each scene, words (in order of relevance) that best describe each scene. **Plenary** Discuss the types of words used to describe the moods in each scene and the children's reasons for choosing them.	discuss strategies to spell the polysyllabic words on the interactive activity by syllabifying, identifying rules

DAY 3 ■ Comparing themes

Key features	Stages	Additional opportunities
Enquiry: compare how a theme is presented in prose, poetry and other media	**Introduction** Identify with the children the main themes in other texts studied, for example *The Lottie Project, The Ghost of Thomas Kempe*. Ask the children to explain how these themes were portrayed through the narrative, through the action and description and behaviour of characters. Remind them of key scenes, for example when Lottie gives Jamie a cake with *I like you* on it, or when Thomas Kempe meets James in his room. (See CD-ROM.) Explain to the children that they are going to look at how a theme is presented in a film. Show them *The Piano* again and ask them to write down on their individual whiteboards what they think the theme is. After viewing the film, take feedback and record ideas on a flipchart.	
	Independent work Divide the children into groups of four and provide each child with a copy of photocopiable page 95 'Comparing themes'. Ask each one of the children in the group to focus on each of the areas identified. Show the film again and tell the children to record their observations on the back of the sheet. Ensure that they identify all aspects.	**Extend:** identify different techniques used in the film to tell the story
	Plenary Take feedback from all of the groups and record their ideas on a board. Encourage the children to deduce how the film director, like the writer, creates the theme by combining the ideas together.	**Support:** focus on what the main character does and how he is feeling

DAY 4 ■ Describing a scene

Key features	Stages	Additional opportunities
	Introduction Show the children only the opening scene of the film again (man playing piano on his own). Ask the children to describe the mood. Remind them of the discussion that took place on Day 1 regarding what they thought he would be thinking about as he played. Remind them also of the techniques used by the film maker that they recorded yesterday. Note the children's ideas on a board. Using shared writing and the ideas on the board, draft with the children an entry for the main character's diary. Use the following as a starting line *As I sit at the piano and play that old, old tune...* As the text develops, discuss with the children different ways of ordering the words in the sentences to ensure that the correct atmosphere is created with the words that link to the film's opening sequence.	link to knowledge of the second world war
Creative thinking: describing a scene in own words	**Independent work** Ask the children to write their own descriptions of the opening scene, using the skills outlined in the modelled session. Remind them that they need to convey in words what the film director has created with images.	**Extend:** focus on the use of descriptive language in their own writing and compare the opening of the film with the opening of a book
	Plenary Play the scene again and read some examples of the children's work. Discuss how closely the descriptions came to accurately reflecting the mood and character seen on screen.	**Support:** provide a simple frame for diary writing

Guided reading

Read a wide range of fiction texts that have film adaptations, for example *The Lion, the Witch and the Wardrobe*, *Stormbreaker*.

As the children read, discuss how the film versions differ from the written. Highlight changes that have been made and make inferences about why these decisions were taken.

Assessment

During the oral sessions, make simple assessments of children's ability to identify with the film narrative.

Focus on how the boys engage with texts and their abilities to infer and deduce from the film text.

Refer back to the learning outcomes on page 85.

Further work

Encourage the children to look at film versions of narrative texts that are familiar to them and identify differences in how they are presented, for example *The Railway Children*, *Harry Potter*.

DAY 1 Creating a background story

Key features	Stages	Additional opportunities
Empathy: reflect on how working in role helps to explore complex issues	**Introduction** Tell the children that they are going to use some dramatic techniques to explore some of the ideas behind the story in *The Piano*. Use the technique of teacher in role to explore these ideas. Use a small prop such as a hat or coat to create the character for the children. Explain that at a certain point, such as when you pick up the prop or put the coat on, you are now in role as the man in the film. **Speaking and listening** In pairs, ask the children to think of questions that they would like to ask the main character. Play the film for them again and then provide the children with a back story to the character's history explaining why those memories were significant to him. Ensure you discuss all the significant memories. Then allow the children to ask you their questions while you are in role. **Independent work** Begin to model for the children a first person account that explains what the memories are and why they are so significant. Ask the children to choose one of the significant moments to write about. They should write their own diary entries in the first person. Use the following as a starting sentence *I remember the day I got the hobby horse.* **Plenary** Select one or two examples of the children's writing to read out to the class. Discuss with the children how they have conveyed the main character's thoughts via the writing.	remind the children of the rules for first and third person **Extend:** provide as much detail in their diary entry as possible **Support:** provide simple question starters, for example *Who is the man who is killed? Where were you?*

DAY 2 Writing narrative and dialogue

Key features	Stages	Additional opportunities
	Introduction Replay a scene from the film as a starting point for stimulating discussion, for example the scene of the woman and the man playing the piano. Discuss with the children whether she is a ghost and what the significance of playing the piano together was for the characters. Discuss with children what she might be saying to him as she leaves him. Remind the children of the conventions of writing dialogue (see Narrative Unit 1). Model for the children a possible narrative for the scene including the conversation between the man and the woman.	
Creative thinking: write own narrative and dialogue in third person	**Independent work** Invite the children to write their own narrative balanced with dialogue for the scene with the man and woman at the piano. Ask them to write in the third person creating a strong narrative voice that sets the mood of the writing, for example *The couple had always played together. Now he was alone he had nothing but his memories...* **Plenary** Share one or two of the children's texts with the class. Discuss how the writing is a balance between the narrative description and the conversation between the two characters. Play the scene from the film, this time without the sound track. As you do so, read an example of the children's writing and discuss whether the content of the dialogue reflects the mood of the images on screen.	**Extend:** focus on correct punctuation of dialogue **Support:** provide a simple writing frame to help write the narrative

DAY 3 ■ Creating a dialogue

Key features	Stages	Additional opportunities
	Introduction Return to the film and select different images that suggest dialogue between two characters, for example when man and woman are together at the piano, the man and his friend, the present being given, the man and the boy together at the piano. Explain to the children that they are going to write the dialogue for the characters at different points in the film.	
	Speaking and listening Ask the children, in pairs, to role play the conversation between two of the characters. They should use the five Ws (who, what, where why and when) to ensure that they have created a context for their scenes. The children should make sure that the characters they are role playing are distinct via their posture, gesture and tone of voice.	**Extend:** record dialogue with reporting clauses including an action starting with *as*, for example: *cried Sarah as she ran away*
Reasoning: to apply knowledge of punctuation of dialogue to own writing	**Independent work** Use shared writing to remind the children how to punctuate dialogue on the run. Repeat the process for one or two other examples of dialogue. Recap on the correct punctuation of dialogue and how to vary reporting clauses, for example adverbs, powerful verbs, action. Ask them to record the conversations they imagine to take place for two of the other scenes.	**Support:** provide speech bubbles for children to record conversations
	Plenary Ask the children to create oral voiceovers for different scenes in the film. Run the film with the children providing the dialogue between the characters.	

Guided reading

Continue to read a number of different stories that have been adapted for the screen. Focus on passages that have conversations between the characters. Discuss the following:
■ how dialogue is interspersed with action and narration
■ how different characters' words are punctuated
■ the variety of reporting clauses.

Assessment

Informally assess children's ability to write dialogue accurately by using the following criteria:
■ each person who speaks is written on a separate line
■ punctuation within speech marks
■ reporting clauses varied, sometimes with precise verbs, other times with adverbs
■ sometimes the reporting clause has an action starting with *as*.
Refer back to the learning outcomes on page 85.

Further work

The children convert their dialogue into first person narrative using a balance between direct and reported speech.

DAY 1 ■ Different narrative structures

Key features	Stages	Additional opportunities
Enquiry: compare different types of narrative and how they are structured	### Introduction Remind the children of the common narrative structure, which is in linear form. Recap on the sequence of events in a known story. Record the main events on a line. Show children *The Piano* again and ask them to note down on their individual whiteboards the sequence of events. Explain to the children that this structure is known as a flashback but it still tells a story. Record the flashback events with the children in the order that they occur (see photocopiable page 96 'Narrative sequence' for details). With the children, think about what possible questions are raised by the flashback sequences but are not answered by the film's events, for example: Who was the friend that died? How long had the man known him? Where was he when it happened? Explain that the director left these things unanswered so that the viewer could answer these questions themselves. ### Independent work Provide the children with copies photocopiable page 96. Ask them to create sequences of chronological events from the flashback sequences. Which events in the film would come first? Ask the children to cut up the statements and put them in order, then to think about the questions that are left unanswered by the film. ### Plenary Discuss the effectiveness of the flashback sequence in telling the story. Compare this with the chronological sequence the children have made.	show the children how authors suggest things are going to happen by giving hints **Extend:** children write questions about the characters that they want answered **Support:** support children in sequencing the story in chronological order

DAY 2 ■ Creating a character

Key features	Stages	Additional opportunities
	### Introduction Draw on the board a grid that is an enlarged version of photocopiable page 97 'Your character'. Show the children three props, for example a picture, a box, a book. Discuss these with the children and begin to build up, through discussion, a character's personality and why these items are significant to him or her. Ask the children: *When might this have been given to him/her? Why might it have become really important to him/her?* Ask the children to build up the stories around the items, recording their ideas on their individual whiteboards. Take feedback from the children. Show how, together, you have created a character's personality and events in their life through thinking around the items. Begin to model for the children a diary entry from the character about one of the items. Show the children how, because it is a diary, they can write very personal memories. Discuss how they can draw upon their own experiences to write. ### Independent work Provide the children with copies of photocopiable page 97 and ask them first to create their character, thinking of the significant items, and then write a short diary extract about the circumstances surrounding one of them. ### Plenary Take feedback and discuss the diary entries with the class.	**Extend:** children write a detailed description of their character **Support:** write a wanted poster that describes their character
Creative thinking: create own story character		

DAY 3 ■ Making a storyboard

Key features	Stages	Additional opportunities
Creative thinking: experiment with different narrative and information texts to write their own stories	**Introduction** Draw a three-by-three grid that resembles photocopiable page 98 'Flashback storyboard' on the board. Explain to the children that they are going to plan their own flashback story using the storyboard technique. Tell them that story boarding (that is, drawing pictures and thinking about the angles that images are taken from) are how films start. Return to the grid and explain that they are going to plan a flashback sequence using the ideas they created yesterday. Ask the children to think of an activity that their character might be doing when he or she thinks about the significant items that they identified on Day 2, for example writing, listening to music, reading, sitting in a chair. Sketch these positions, discussing angles for the pictures and then drawing the pictures of the items in the smaller flashback boxes. **Independent work** Provide the children with copies of photocopiable page 98. Ask them to identify which of the three items would be in the first flashback sequence, the second and so forth. Remind them that they need to consider the angles that they want to draw the shots from. **Plenary** Tell the children to share their storyboards, explaining the flashback sequences, discussion angles and different types of shot. During the plenary, explain to children that on Day 5 they are going to create their own pictures using digital photographs and models to sequence their story.	**Extend:** draw a series of different angles their character could be shot from **Support:** provide figures and a setting so that they can place their characters at different angles and sketch them

DAY 4 ■ Guess my word!

Key features	Stages	Additional opportunities
Information processing: guessing words by analysing clues	**Introduction** Play 'Guess my word' with the children by providing them with a number of different clues as to the content of the word. For example, for magician: ■ This word has three syllables. ■ It has the suffix -cian at the end. ■ Its root word has five phonemes ■ The last middle phoneme should make a g sound but makes a j instead. ■ It means a person who plays tricks. Provide the children with a number of different words ending with suffixes, for example *complexion, optician, electrician, session, confusion, completion, fiction, direction*. Ask them to create the clues to spell the words and then try them out on each other. **Independent work** Write three different sentences on a board, for example *The old man went down the road. He went to the shop. He chose a book.* Ask the children to improve the sentences by adding: more precise nouns, a range of adverbs, and conjunctions. Extend the children's challenge by asking them to turn the sentence into a sentence found in an information book, a novel, a set of instructions and so on. **Plenary** Discuss how the sentence types change according to the kind of text.	**Extend:** remember spellings by using a variety of strategies **Support:** use spelling lists to secure accurate spelling of key words

DAY 5 ■ Shooting the story

Key features	Stages	Additional opportunities
Creative thinking: use ICT equipment to create and present flashback sequences	### Introduction Return the children to their completed versions of photocopiable page 98 'Flashback storyboard'. Explain to them that they are going to create their images using figures and backdrops that they have made, (or alternatively they could get classmates to act as models). Remind them that they need to make sure that the items that were significant for each flashback sequence are clearly identifiable against the scene they are creating. Using a digital camera or web cam show the children how to take pictures from different angles. Remind them to create a scene with their main character in the present so that they can use this as the scene to flashback from. ### Independent work Invite the children to set up their own scenes with their figures and settings (or classmates as models). They should create three flashback scenes where they show the significance of the items in their plan. Remind the children that they can take the photos themselves. ### Plenary At the end of the session, ask the children to import their photos onto a computer and check that they have got all the shots they wanted. Share the photos with the class and discuss how effective they are in portraying flashback sequences.	**Link to art:** the children could create their own figures and sets for their characters, for example with card, boxes **Extend:** children take more than one picture from different angles and select the best **Support:** take one picture of each scene from their storyboard

DAY 5 ■ Creating a multimedia presentation

Key features	Stages	Additional opportunities
Creative thinking: use a range of ICT programs to present and create texts	### Introduction Using a multimedia presentation program, for example PowerPoint® or Microsoft Photo Story 3®. Model for the children how to insert their images into the program to create a storyboard. From there, show them how to create transitions between one or more of the pictures to create a multimedia presentation. If using PowerPoint®, show the children how they can intersperse the images of their scenes with a slide with words – like a silent film. ### Independent work Ask the children, in pairs or individually, depending on access to computers, to create their own small film or multimedia presentation using the images they have taken with the digital camera or web cam. Ensure that they have made clear transitions between flashback images and the present day images, using the facilities in the programs they are working with. ### Plenary Invite the children to play their films/photo presentations and compare them against their story-board versions. Discuss how the flashbacks have been created and how clearly each of the significant items have been shown.	**Extend:** children write a paragraph evaluating their multimedia presentation **Support:** help the children to order the events in their story chronologically

DAY 7 ■ Writing a flashback story

Key features	Stages	Additional opportunities
	Introduction Using one of the children's presentations and storyboards as an example, model for the class how to create a flashback story in written narrative form. Remind them that they have already made some written examples of film narrative, for example, Phase 1, Day 4, and Phase 3, Day 3. Explain that when writing they should include all the details that have been suggested in their film or photo presentation. Model for the children the first paragraph where they introduced the character (refer them back to the notes made on photocopiable page 97 'Your character'). Demonstrate how by paragraphing they can create the flashback. Show the children how they can use a variety of techniques such as ellipses or a connecting sentence to signal to the reader that the flashback is going to occur.	
Enquiry: experiment with different narrative forms and styles to write own stories		**Extend:** the children write a further one or two paragraphs
	Independent work Tell the children write to their own narrative of their storyboard. Limit them to writing perhaps three paragraphs, that is the opening, the first flashback and then the return to the present.	**Support:** provide a writing frame that helps structure the flashback sequence
	Plenary Ask the children to read their written narratives alongside their multimedia versions. Discuss the differing strengths and weaknesses of the multimedia narrative and the written narrative.	

Guided reading
Read with the children examples of texts that follow different narrative patterns, for example flashbacks or parallel stories, see *Kensuke's Kingdom* by Michael Morpurgo or *The Lottie Project* by Jacqueline Wilson .

Assessment
Assess the children's understanding of the visual/film narrative by assessing their images created for the film. Use the assessment sheet 'Sorting and writing' from the CD-ROM to assess the children's understanding of narrative structure using flashbacks. Refer back to the learning outcomes on page 85.

Further work
Provide further time for the children to develop their models for the scenes so that they are of high quality.

Comparing themes

Camera angles

Look for:

■ Where the camera points (low, high, above, at the side).

■ Close up or wide angle.

Lighting

Look for:

■ How scenes are lit such as spotlight.

■ Shadows.

■ Reflections.

■ Use of colour – shades or tones.

Music

Listen for:

■ Patterns.

■ Change of sound or tune.

■ Different tones hi or low.

Movement, scenes and expressions

Look for:

■ How the character's expression changes.

■ How scenes change and flashbacks are created.

Illustrations © Nova Developments.

Name _____   Date _____

Narrative sequence

The narrative sequence shown in the film

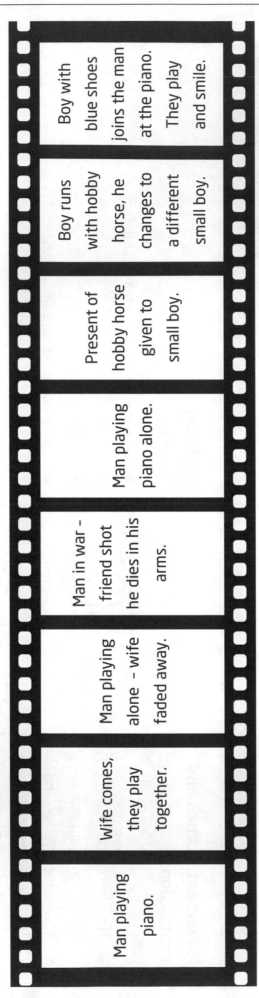

| Man playing piano. | Wife comes, they play together. | Man playing alone – wife faded away. | Man in war – friend shot he dies in his arms. | Man playing piano alone. | Present of hobby horse given to small boy. | Boy runs with hobby horse, he changes to a different small boy. | Boy with blue shoes joins the man at the piano. They play and smile. |

Chronological sequence

■ Cut out these statements and place them in the order that you think they might have happened in the main character's life.

		Wife playing with him at the piano.
	Friend being shot.	Small boy with blue shoes playing with hobby horse.
Boy running and playing with the hobby horse.	Boy and man playing together, smiling.	
Man joining the army hospital in the war.	Man playing the piano.	
Present of a hobby horse.		
Wife leaving him/ dying.		

PHOTOCOPIABLE   ■SCHOLASTIC
www.scholastic.co.uk

Name _____

Date _____

Your character

■ Draw in each box one thing that represents an important memory for your character.

Item 1	Item 2	Item 3

■ Underneath each picture explain briefly why it is important to your character, where he/she got it and when in his life he got it.

_____

_____

_____

■ Write brief details about your character describe:

The kind of clothes he/she wears _____

How he/she walks and talks – mannerisms _____

Words or phrases he/she likes to say _____

Hobbies or interests he/she has _____

Name _____   Date _____

Flashback storyboard

■ Plan your own story using this sheet. Remember to consider where your character is and what they are doing and how scenes change.

Present

Flashback
■ What is significant about the flashback?
■ What memory are we going back to?

Present
■ How does the expression on the main character's face change?

Flashback

Flashback
■ Where does it take place?
■ What happens?

Present
■ Show your character with a different expression or action.

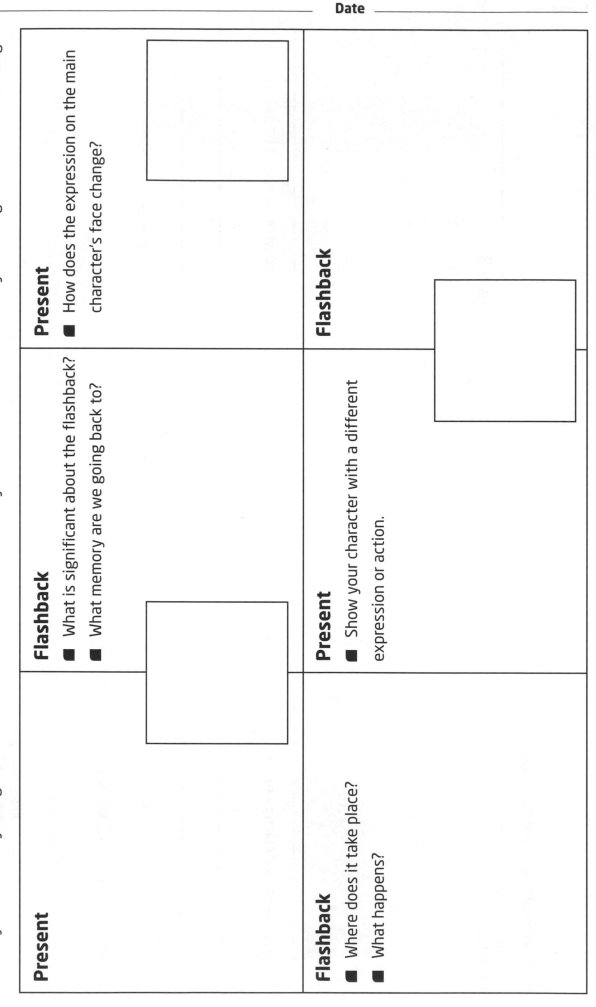

■ 100 LITERACY FRAMEWORK LESSONS YEAR 5

PHOTOCOPIABLE

■ SCHOLASTIC
www.scholastic.co.uk

NARRATIVE
UNIT 6 Dramatic conventions

Speak and listen for a range of purposes on paper and on screen

Strand 1 Speaking
- Present a spoken argument, sequencing points logically, defending views with evidence and making use of persuasive language.

Strand 2 Listening and responding
- Identify some aspects of talk that vary between formal and informal occasions.

Strand 3 Group discussion and interaction
- Plan and manage a group task over time using different levels of planning.
- Understand different ways to take the lead and support others in groups.

Strand 4 Drama
- Perform a scripted scene making use of dramatic conventions.
- Use and recognise the impact of theatrical effects in drama.

Read for a range of purposes on paper and on screen

Strand 6 Word structure and spelling
- Spell words containing unstressed vowels.
- Know and use less common prefixes and suffixes such as *im-, ir-, -cian*.
- Group and classify words according to their spelling patterns and their meanings.

Strand 7 Understanding and Interpreting texts
- Compare different types of narrative and information texts and identify how they are structured.
- Explore how writers use language for comic and dramatic effects.

Strand 8 Engaging with and responding to texts
- Compare how a common theme is presented in poetry, prose and other media.

Write for a range of purposes on paper and on screen

Strand 9 Creating and shaping texts
- Reflect independently and critically on their own writing and edit and improve it.
- Adapt non-narrative forms and styles to write fiction or factual texts, including poems.

Strand 10 Text structure and organisation
- Experiment with the order of sections and paragraphs to achieve different effects.

Strand 11 Sentence structure and punctuation
- Adapt sentence construction to different text-types, purposes and readers.
- Punctuate sentences accurately, including using speech marks and apostrophes.

Strand 12 Presentation
- Use a range of ICT programs to present texts, making informed choices about which electronic tools to use for different purposes.

Progression in narrative

In this year, children are moving towards:
- Analysing the structure of more complex narratives; looking at the way that

▶

UNIT 6 ◄ Dramatic Conventions *continued*

the author signals a change in the narration and discuss the effect of seeing the story from different points of view.

■ Making inferences about the perspective of the author from what is written and what is implied; exploring ways to change the narrative viewpoint.

■ Recognising that characters may have different perspectives on the story and explore different points of view; reviewing ways to vary pace by using direct or reported speech at different points in a story.

■ Writing in the style of a particular author to complete a section of a story, add dialogue or a new chapter.

■ Planning and writing a longer story with a more complex structure. Experiment with the order of chapters or paragraphs to achieve different effects; using dialogue to build character.

■ Checking for consistency in narrative voice when telling each part of a story.

Key aspects of learning covered in this Unit

Enquiry
Children will ask questions relating to the theme of their scripted presentation, research the relevant content and then plan how to present that content effectively.

Information processing
Children will identify relevant information from a range of sources on paper and on screen and use this to write their scripts.

Evaluation
Children will discuss success criteria, give feedback to others and judge the effectiveness of their own work.

Communication
Children will develop their ability to analyse and evaluate a range of scripted broadcasts. They will learn how to plan and create a script, including the use of script writing conventions.

Prior learning

Before starting this Unit check that the children understand:

■ Plays are divided into sections called scenes

■ The setting is often briefly described at the beginning of a scene.

■ Every speech by a character starts on a new line.

■ Each speech starts with the character's name.

■ Speeches are not punctuated with speech marks.

■ Stage directions are used to show actions or how characters are to speak.

■ Stage directions may be written in brackets or italics.

■ Characters arriving and leaving are described as entrances and exits.

If they need further support please refer to a prior Unit or a similar Unit in Year 4.

Resources

The wrong bag by Campbell Perry ✺; Audio *The News* by Isabel Macdonald ✺ *News transcript* by Isabel Macdonald ✺; Persuasion skeleton ✺; Photocopiable pages 112 'Audience cards'; Photocopiable page 113 'Different question types'; Photocopiable page 114 'Planning an interview'; Assessment activity 'Working in a group 1' ✺

Cross-curricular opportunities

History

UNIT 6 ■ Teaching sequence

Phase	Children's objectives	Summary of activities	Learning outcomes
1	I can compare different types of narrative texts and identify how they are structured. I can spell words containing unstressed vowels. I can adapt sentence construction of broadcast news to different audiences. I can use and recognise the impact of theatrical effects in drama.	Read and listen to two examples of scripts from the CD-ROM. *The wrong bag* and *The News* (audio). Children make adaptations to *News transcript* on CD-ROM using photocopiable page 112. Identify common spelling patterns in words with unstressed vowels. Use *The wrong bag* and the *News transcript* to explore differences between the two scripts.	Children can identified differences between written plays, scripts and oral news. Children can understand rules for spelling words containing unstressed vowels and change writing to suit different audiences. Children can understand the different dramatic strategies for news broadcasts and plays.
2	I can understand some aspects of talk that vary between formal and informal situations. I know and use the less common prefixes and suffixes. I can adapt sentence construction to different text types. I can present a spoken argument making use of persuasive language.	Use web-based material to discuss similarities and differences between performances, scripts and so on. Children adapt a paragraph of the *News transcript* for different audiences. Children learn the prefixes *im-, in-, ir-*. Create own persuasive argument. Use persuasion skeleton on CD-ROM to structure argument.	Children can identify similarities and differences between interviews and television bulletins. Children know the rules for spelling words containing less common prefixes. Children can write persuasive argument written for an issue relating to school.
3	I can explore how writers use language for comic and dramatic effect. I can adapt sentence construction to different text types, purposes and readers. I can identify some aspects of talk that vary between formal and informal.	Identify difference between language features of different broadcasts and techniques. Children write own news script with three stories, using class activities as a basis for writing. Identify strategies for interviewing. Use web-based interviews.	Children can identify language features of news. Children can write a news script containing three stories, applying features identified. Children can produce a checklist of interviewing techniques.
4	I can plan and manage a group task over time using different levels of planning. I can understand the different ways to take the lead and support others in a group. I can adapt non-narrative forms and styles to write fiction or factual texts. I can perform a scripted scene making use of dramatic conventions. I can use a range of ICT programs to present texts. I can reflect independently and critically on writing.	Use group work to create school news. Children use photocopiable page 114. Children identify key people to interview for the broadcast, conduct interview and film with digital video. Children draft the news script collaboratively. Children identify where to include the interview footage. Children rehearse the broadcast and then record it, using digital video, tape or MP3 recorder. Using Windows Movie Maker®, collate and edit the complete news broadcast. Children evaluate the scripts and films created, and group work.	Children can create a plan for a group task and write potential questions planned for interviewees. Children can conduct interviews recorded on video, as a group task. Children can draft a script of news stories written and ready for recording. Children can create a digital video file of news broadcast. Children can create collated news and interview footage. Children can evaluate broadcasts, and scripts and the group work.

Provide copies of the objectives for the children.

DAY 1 ■ Different types of script

Key features	Stages	Additional opportunities
Enquiry: investigating the structure of scripts	**Introduction** Use the playscript *The wrong bag* from the CD-ROM to remind the children of the dramatic conventions that are identifiable in a script. Explain how playscripts are similar to the narrative form of a story, but they tell the story through live action and dialogue instead of through words. Identify with the children some of the features, for example stage directions; instructions for the scene and how the stage should be set; there is a cast and so on. Ask the children to think of examples of texts or broadcasts that require a script, for example public speeches, presentations, radio and television reports, television programmes, television and radio advertisements. Play *The news* audio file from the CD-ROM. Ask the children to listen carefully to the text as it is read. How do they think that the reader knows what to say? How is the information organised? Then discuss punctuation, complex sentences and conjunctions and how these are used in scripts.	**Extend:** children listen to *The news* again and write as many conjunctions that they can hear
	Independent work Ask the children to work in pairs and to list the key features of scripts. They should think about how a news script differs from a playscript. Give the children copies of *The wrong bag and* ask them to discuss and highlight its key features as a script.	**Support:** provide simpler conjunctions, to listen out for when listening to *The news* audio file
	Plenary As a class, discuss the paired work and provide feedback.	

DAY 2 ■ Different audiences

Key features	Stages	Additional opportunities
	Introduction Discuss with the children the potential different audiences for a news broadcast. Ask how the writing and tone of the broadcast would be different for different audiences. Using the *News transcript* from the CD-ROM discuss with the children possible changes to the first paragraph that would need to be made if the audience was a group of infant children. Highlight to children that they need to make changes to the sentence construction, vocabulary, tenses and so on. Annotate and make changes.	**Extend:** children identify what they changed and why it was suitable for the audience
Information processing: adapt sentence construction to different text types, purposes and readers	**Speaking and listening** Provide the children with copies of the 'Audience cards' on photocopiable page 112 and copies of the *News transcript*. Ask them to make changes to the script for the second paragraph of the news for the different audiences.	**Support:** provide simple sentences that are aimed at different audiences for children to sort
	Plenary Invite the children to read out the changes to the transcript. Discuss the changes that were made and the reasons for these changes.	

DAY 3 ■ Playscripts and news broadcasting

Key features	Stages	Additional opportunities
	### Introduction Provide the children with copies of *The wrong bag* and the *News transcript* from the CD-ROM. Discuss the differing techniques that will enable these to be performed effectively. Take suggestions from the children and record their different ideas on a board divided into two columns: 'playscript' and 'news file'. Discuss why the news needs to be written in script form.	
Communication: working in a group to perform different types of script	### Independent work Divide the children into groups of four and explain that they are going to explore the different performance techniques that they need to employ if they are to act out *The wrong bag* or read the *News transcript* effectively. Give the children sufficient time to work on their performances. Then bring the class together to share their performances. Ask the children to explain the different strategies they have had to use in order to perform the scene or read the news. Appoint a scribe for each group to record these strategies on a group whiteboard. Some examples they could record are: slow reading, change of tone, listening to another person's line for a cue, creating a tone of voice from a stage cue and so on.	make short assessment observations of different children and how they work together as a group
	### Plenary Select groups of children to perform their interpretation of both the *News transcript* and *The wrong bag*. Invite them to explain the dramatic techniques that they have used (those that they recorded on their whiteboard) and transfer these to the class chart created in the introduction.	

Guided reading
Read a range of plays with the children, discussing ways of showing the characters and the different clues in the text which show where the scene takes place, how the characters are speaking and so on. Encourage the children also to discuss what is implied in these situations.

Assessment
Use informal assessment procedures to make notes about key children's ability to work in a group situation. Identify the following. Ability to:
- turn take
- negotiate
- collaborate
- work co-operatively.

Refer back to the learning outcomes on page 101.

Further work
Encourage the children to look and listen carefully to different examples of broadcasting on the television and radio. Encourage them to identify the different types of scripts that are needed.

DAY 1 ▪ Comparing different broadcast material

Key features	Stages	Additional opportunities
Enquiry: identify different types of broadcast	**Introduction** For this lesson use the internet to find different examples of broadcast material, such as news reports, interviews, weather broadcasts, advertisements and so on. View each of the broadcasts in turn and discuss with the children the following key questions: ■ Why would a script be needed? ■ What evidence is there that there is a script? ■ What type of language does the interview use? Formal or informal? **Independent work** Write the following criteria on a board or flipchart to help structure children's viewing of each clip. How does the interviewer phrase the questions? What types of questions do they use? How does the reporter talk to the camera/audience? Is the language they use formal or informal? What evidence is there that they have planned what they are going to say? View each broadcast separately via the internet and ask the children in pairs to record notes about the differences between them on their individual whiteboards. **Plenary** As a whole class draw together the variety of techniques that they have observed for making different types of broadcasts. Create a list on a white-board with children's help and input.	**Extend:** the children compare two interviews and the differences between them, focusing on the language used **Support:** when watching broadcasts, give children one or two key ideas to look for

DAY 2 ▪ Changing the script

Key features	Stages	Additional opportunities
Information processing: rewriting paragraphs in a script	**Introduction** Show the children a list of words on the board including the following: *inactive, irresponsible, immature, indecent, incapable, impossible, impolite, impatient.* Ask the children to identify what the words have in common. Agree that these prefixes mean 'not', and that when *ir-* is added to a word starting with *r*, doubles the *r*. **Speaking and listening** Ask the children to work in pairs and identify some strategies for remembering how to spell the words: syllabification, root word, prefix. **Independent work** Return the children to the audience cards and the *News transcript* that they used on Phase 1, Day 2. Remind them of the changes they made to the script. Ask them to choose two different audiences from the cards and to rewrite the original paragraph for these two audiences. **Plenary** Take feedback and discuss the changes the children made to the paragraph for the two different audiences, highlighting the changes made.	**Extend:** identify two more audiences and change the paragraphs accordingly **Support:** in a guided group, change one paragraph for a specific audience

DAY 3 ■ Planning an argument

Key features	Stages	Additional opportunities
	### Introduction Using the techniques identified during the previous lesson, explain to the children that they are going to present an oral argument that is designed to persuade children that it is a good idea to join in the *Walk to School* project (www.walktoschool.org). Show them the Persuasion skeleton from the CD-ROM. Talk about the points that they need to make in order to persuade others to walk to school, for example they will get to school on time as they won't get caught in traffic jams. Tell the children that they will need to rehearse their arguments. Remind them that they need to be as persuasive as possible in their arguments and the manner in which they argue, so they will need to consider their audience. What would appeal to or persuade Year 5 children, for example? Can they think of a jingle or catch phrase that would appeal to the audience and so on?	**Extend:** ensure children include different connectives in spoken arguments
	### Independent work Split the children into pairs or groups. Print out the persuasion skeleton from the CD-ROM for each group. They should use this to help plan out their arguments. Allow them time to rehearse their arguments and plan their presentations.	**Support:** encourage the use of full and extended sentences
Evaluation: evaluating each other's arguments	### Plenary Ask each of the groups to present their arguments to the rest of the class. Ask the audience to provide feedback on the effectiveness of the their arguments.	

Guided reading
Encourage the children to read and watch a range of material that includes broadcast news. Discuss and reinforce with the children the various techniques used to create the different pieces.

Assessment
Make informal assessments of the children's ability to put ideas together so that they form a coherent argument and to back up and reinforce their points.
Refer back to the learning outcomes on page 101.

Further work
Revise different types of connectives used in persuasive language.

DAY 1 ◼ Language in broadcast script writing

Key features	Stages	Additional opportunities
Enquiry: looking at language in scripts and evaluating effectiveness	### Introduction Provide the children with copies of the *News transcript* from the CD-ROM and, through shared reading, identify and record on the board the different features of the language used, for example person, tense, sentence structure, summary sentences and so on. Discuss how the news has been put together. What was each of the stories about? Why did the news writer put them together in that way? Explain that in a newsroom all the different stories come in and the editor chooses what order to put them in. If the main story is a serious one then he or she will choose a lighter story to end with. Explore with the children the effects of putting the stories in different order by moving the text around. Discuss how the language used for each story reflects the mood of it and whether it is serious or light-hearted. ### Speaking and listening Ask the children to listen to and watch different examples of news reports via the internet. They should listen out for the different language techniques used. Ask them to identify the different stories covered and record any words or phrases they think are particularly effective on their individual whiteboards. ### Plenary Discuss and take brief feedback from the children's observations. As a class, put together some key tips for putting together news scripts. Keep this list for Day 2.	**Extend:** encourage the children to identify different styles of reporting **Support:** provide a simple checklist of key features to look for in a news report

DAY 2 ◼ Year 5 news

Key features	Stages	Additional opportunities
	### Introduction Explain to the children that they are now going to practise writing their own Year 5 news script. Discuss potential news stories with the children. Establish who the potential audience for this writing would be, for example parents, children, teachers, governors. Together create a list of different newsworthy stories about the class, such as achievements in swimming; holidays taken; personal achievements; class or school events that they have taken part in such as concerts, school plays, sports events and so on. When the list has been created, discuss the three stories they want to take on and how the tone of each should be different. ### Independent work Either in pairs or individually, ask the children to create their three-story news script. Provide the children with a deadline, that the news has to be read out, for example three o'clock. Make the list of features (made on Day 1) available for the children as a reminder.	**Extend:** children write a variety of different headlines for the story and discuss the best one **Support:** provide a simple writing frame to assist with writing the new story
Evaluation: write own news story and evaluate it	### Plenary Invite the children to read out their news stories. Then discuss how effective the stories were and the features they included.	

DAY 3 ■ Conducting an effective interview

Key features	Stages	Additional opportunities
Enquiry: investigating different question types	### Introduction Explain to the children that they are going to look closely at interviewing techniques. Tell them that this is preparation for next week's work, where they will interview people and then create their own news bulletin. Use one or two interviews, found via the internet, for example an interview of Jacqueline Wilson or another author or celebrity that the children are familiar with. ### Speaking and listening Allow the children initially just to watch the clips to get a sense of the context. Then divide the children into pairs and ask one person to listen to and write down all the different types of questions that are asked, while the other listens to the responses and notes down how long or short they are. After viewing, take feedback from the children and identify which questions got the best responses. Highlight the differences between formal and informal language in the interviews. Use photocopiable page 113 'Different question types', to outline for children the different question types and discuss which were used in the clips and which were most effective. Give the children copies of the photocopiable so they can categorise the questions. ### Plenary As a class, discuss the question types they categorised using the photocopiable sheet. Then review one of the clips again, this time focusing on the responses to the questions.	**Extend:** discuss why reporters need to have planned their questions and why these would need to use more formal language **Support:** children think of different questions and identify if they are open, closed or probing

Guided reading
Encourage the children to read as widely as possible from a number of different contemporary authors.
Discuss with them the different genres of narrative texts including structures of these types. Discuss favourites.

Assessment
Informally assess the children's ability to write effectively in short spaces of time.
Focus attention on the children's grammatical constructions and sentence punctuation in your marking to identify key areas to work on in the coming weeks.
Refer back to the learning outcomes on page 101.

Further work
Ask children to practice interviewing each other about personal interests. Identify why it is important to have prepared their questions beforehand.
Encourage them to identify where they have used different question types.

DAY 1 ■ Planning school news

Key features	Stages	Additional opportunities
Communication: plan a news broadcast while working in a group	**Introduction** The next lessons involve the children, in groups, writing and preparing a six-story news item which will be recorded digitally. Prepare in advance potential stories that the children could include in their news. Try to make these as topical as possible, relating to events in the school. Explain to the children that they are going to make their own broadcast news using digital video and Windows Movie Maker®. If possible, split them into groups of six and explain that their news will need a script, so each member of the group is going to write one of the six stories. (Make sure each child in a group covers a different story.) Allow the children to choose which person is going to cover which story. **Independent work** Invite the children to begin planning their individual stories. Ask them to consider the following: What facts have they got about it? Who they might interview? What questions might they ask? Provide them with a deadline for the end of the session to have established the key facts about the story and who they want to interview, and to have prepared interview questions that all members have agreed on. **Plenary** Discuss with each group their ideas for the news stories and their planning for the interviews. Give appropriate feedback and provide assistance where necessary.	**Extend:** the children list the rules for group collaboration, such as listening, turn taking, negotiating and present these to the class **Support:** support the children in thinking of different types of questions to ask

DAY 2 ■ Making the story

Key features	Stages	Additional opportunities
Communication: begin collating information and filming the interviews for the news broadcast in groups	**Introduction** Explain to the children that they are shortly going to be moving into their news story groups to discuss and agree how they are going to approach the news interviewing. They need to think about: who they are going to interview first; which questions to ask and in what order; who is going to ask them; who is going to film the interview; who is going to record the answers in note form and so on. Remind them that each person needs to be clear about what they are doing. Discuss how they can make notes about the answers to the questions and so on. **Speaking and listening** Give the children copies of photocopiable page 114 'Planning an interview', so they can conduct their interviews. Brief children on the relevant school rules for working outside the classroom. **Independent work** Children film their interviews and make notes on the story. **Plenary** Briefly discuss and review the task and how the effectively the group worked.	remind the children of strategies to use when taking notes, such as bullet points, abbreviations and so on

DAY 3 ■ Drafting the news script

Key features	Stages	Additional opportunities
	### Introduction Prior to this lesson it would be a good idea to create separate news folders for all the different groups on computers. Ensure that each folder contains copies of the digital video files of the six interviews that the children conducted. Also ensure that every child has a copy of the notes taken at the interview for their story. Gather all of the children together at the start of the session. Explain that this is the time when the news script needs to be written. Ensure that the children are in their groups. Remind them that they have six different stories, so each child in the group can write the part of the news script that relates to the story they worked on. Explain that each news story should include a clip of the interview, which they will need to select. Model the starting point of a news script if necessary.	**Extend:** appoint one child in each group to be editor and collate the different scripts of the story together and edit them if appropriate
Communication: work in a group to write a news script and put together a broadcast	### Independent work Provide a time limit for writing each news script. If appropriate, encourage the children to write it on screen. If facilities are limited, they can hand write it. ### Speaking and listening Provide the children with time to look at the video footage of the interviews filmed. Ask them to appoint a time keeper and for each group to view each interview. Ask them to identify which part they think they want for their clip. ### Plenary Tell the children to agree the order of their stories for the bulletin and practise reading it out loud as if in a news broadcast.	**Support:** provide a writing structure or scaffold to assist with the writing

DAY 4 ■ Recording the news broadcast

Key features	Stages	Additional opportunities
	### Introduction Explain to the children that today they are going to record their news broadcast in their groups. Explain that this is going to be the main piece of film, into which they are going to add the clips they have selected from all the interview footage they made (they will be doing that tomorrow, using Windows Movie Maker®). Remind the children that they will need to make sure that each interview clip is cued so the newsreader knows when to pause. ### Speaking and listening In their groups, ask the children to refine the script and establish a final copy. They decide who is going to be the newsreader. Encourage all of the children to have a go before they make their final decision about who is going to do it.	remind children of the importance of punctuating on the run so their writing makes sense to someone else when they read it
Communication: perform a scripted scene, making use of dramatic conventions	### Independent work The children create their own broadcasting scene with a desk and a chair and film their news, using either a digital video camera or a digital camera with a movie facility. Remind them of the close up facility, eye contact with camera and so on. ### Plenary End the lesson by discussing how the script helped the presenter. Choose some of the groups to present their news orally to the class.	

DAY 5 ■ The final version

Key features	Stages	Additional opportunities
	### Introduction Prior to this lesson, add the digital videos created to each group's folder on the computers. Each folder should now contain seven files: one of newsreading; six of interview footage. Explain to the groups that they are now going to put their news film together. Ask each group to nominate one person to be the director. Explain that in all editing suites there is a director who is in overall charge of the programme. Model for the children how to create the film with Windows Movie Maker®, using one of the group's examples. Ensure that the video files are in the 'my collections' folder within the program. Show the children how they can sequence their film, creating a transition when their interviews come on, and then create their final credit sequence. For more details on using Windows Movie Maker® visit www.microsoft.com/windowsxp/using/moviemaker/default.mspx	
	### Independent work Tell the children to work together editing and collating their news broadcasts. Explain to the groups that all members need to have a go at putting their clip into the collating sequence and choosing the transition sequence they want. Remind them to keep saving and resaving their files. Encourage them to make a rough copy and then refine it.	**Support:** provide children with relevant technical and ICT support where needed
Evaluation: evaluate their efforts in working as a team	### Plenary Discuss briefly with children how effectively they worked together as groups and how they found the task of putting the film together.	

DAY 6 ■ An evaluation

Key features	Stages	Additional opportunities
	### Introduction Tell the children that they are now going to view each group's news broadcast and discuss how effective their scripts and newsreading were. Provide them with a set of distinct criteria on which to evaluate the two areas, the news script and then the broadcast itself. Possible evaluation questions could be: ■ How effectively did the script convey the important ideas in the story? ■ Did the interviewer's questions allow the interviewee to talk at length? ■ Did the interview add to the story and make it stronger? ■ How were the links made by the script to the different interviews? ■ Did the broadcaster speak clearly and vary the tone of his/her voice? Provide these questions to the children on a board and after each group's film has been seen, allow time for discussion. Then allow the group to respond to the evaluation of the other children.	
Evaluation: evaluate their efforts in working as a team and evaluate each other's work	### Independent work Ask all of the children to write a brief summary of each groups broadcast, praising and criticising. When these are completed, ask the children to reform in their original groups and to discuss the comments they made.	**Support:** remind the children of appropriate ways to give feedback in a formal context, such as praising the positive first and then identifying one area to improve
	### Plenary Take general feedback from the children about the task and the evaluations.	

Guided reading

Read with the children examples of texts that have been adapted for the screen for example, the *Harry Potter* series. Discuss why the changes have been made to certain events in the film and so on. Continue to develop the children's ability to discuss the following:

- imagery and word choice
- development of characters
- meanings of vocabulary that is new to children from the context of the sentence
- reading with awareness of punctuation.

Assessment

Informally assess the children's application of ICT skills by observing how they create their own script and they way they manage the Windows Movie Maker® programme.

Informally assess children's ability to work in a group situation. Use the interactive activity 'Working in a group 1' from the CD-ROM to evaluate group work.

Refer back to the learning outcomes on page 101.

Further work

Provide children with opportunities to use ICT, in particular a word processor in another curriculum area, by getting them to write up their scripts electronically. Develop the children's ability to write for different audiences by creating real opportunities to write for both younger and older people.

Audience cards

■ Change the news story for the following audiences.

Audience 1: Children

How I changed the story

Vocabulary:

Length and type of sentences:

Type of facts included:

Audience 2: Grandparents

How I changed the story

Vocabulary:

Length and type of sentences:

Type of facts included:

Audience 3: Teachers

How I changed the story

Vocabulary:

Length and type of sentences:

Type of facts included:

Different question types

- Open questions – designed to get people talking such as *Tell me what you think about...*
- Closed questions – asking something specific such as *Were you frightened?* These limit the responses you get from people – only 'yes' or 'no'
- Probing questions – designed to find out a little bit more about something such as *In that situation did you...?*
- Follow-up question – a second question if the first one doesn't get the answer you want.

Classify the following question types:

Why do you think that homework for primary-aged school children is a good idea?

_____

Where do you live?

_____

You have given your reasons for saying that homework is a good idea, tell me, what did you think of it as a child?

_____

What qualities do you think make a good performer?

_____

How old are you?

_____

You've mentioned three aspects of performance that you think are important, are there any others?

_____

Do you like the new school dinners?

_____

What were the reasons behind improving school dinners?

_____

What foods do you eat and do you consider that they are healthy?

_____

What is your favourite sport at school?

_____

How useful do you consider computers to be to school learners?

_____

We've talked about your views on school dinners, but do you think that they will make children healthier?

_____

NARRATIVE ■ UNIT 6

Planning an interview

The story we are researching is:

These are the facts that we know about this story:

- ■
- ■
- ■
- ■
- ■

People we want to interview are:

1.

2.

Key questions we want to ask: (Remember: open, closed, probing questions.)

- ■
- ■
- ■
- ■
- ■
- ■
- ■
- ■
- ■
- ■

NON-FICTION
UNIT 1 Instructions

Speak and listen for a range of purposes on paper and on screen

Strand 2 Listening and responding
■ Identify some aspects of talk which vary between formal and informal occasions.

Read for a range of purposes on paper and on screen

Strand 6 Word structure and spelling
■ Spell words containing unstressed vowels.
Strand 7 Understanding and interpreting texts
■ Compare different types of narrative and information texts and identify how they are structured.
Strand 8 Engaging with and responding to texts
■ Compare the usefulness of techniques, such as visualisation, prediction, empathy, in exploring the meaning of texts.

Write for a range of purposes on paper and on screen

Strand 9 Creating and shaping texts
■ Reflect independently and critically on own writing and edit and improve it.
■ Adapt non-narrative forms and styles to write fiction or factual texts, including poems.
■ Vary pace and develop viewpoint through the use of direct and reported speech, portrayal of action and selection of detail.
■ Create multi-layered texts, including the use of hyperlinks, linked with web pages.
Strand 10 Text structure and organisation
■ Experiment with the order of sections and paragraphs to achieve different effects.
■ Change the order of material within a paragraph, moving the topic or sentence.
Strand 11 Sentence structure and punctuation
■ Adapt sentence construction to different text-types, purposes and readers.
■ Punctuate sentences accurately, including the use of speech marks and apostrophes.
Strand 12 Presentation
■ Use a range of ICT programs to present texts, making informed choices of which electronic tools to use for different purposes.

Progression in instructions

In this year, children are moving towards:
■ In group work, giving clear oral instructions to achieve the completion of a common task; following oral instructions of increased complexity.
■ Evaluating sets of instructions (including attempting to follow some of them) for purpose, organisation and layout, clarity and usefulness.
■ Identifying sets of instructions which deviate from the norm in terms of structure and language features (for example, recipes).
■ Writing a set of instructions (using appropriate form and features) and testing them out on other people, revising and trying them out again.

▶

Key aspects of learning covered in this Unit

Enquiry
Children will investigate a range of instructional texts by asking relevant questions, researching and following instructions to explore their effectiveness.

Information processing
Children will identify relevant information from a range of sources on paper and on screen and use this as a basis for both oral and written instructions.

Evaluation
Children will read, compare and evaluate instructional texts from a variety of sources. When presenting instructional texts orally and in writing, they will discuss success criteria, give feedback to others and judge the effectiveness of their own work.

Reasoning
Children will draw on their understanding and use of instructional texts to construct reasoned opinions and arguments based on available information and evidence.

Empathy
In discussing and writing about real or simulated events, children will need to imagine themselves in another person's position.

Communication
Children will develop their skills to reflect critically on what they have seen and read. They will develop their ability to give and follow clear instructions and reflect on the effectiveness of different modes of communication. They will work collaboratively in pairs and groups, and outcomes will be both oral and written.

Prior learning

Before starting this Unit check that the children can:
- Recall the language features and organisation of instructional texts.
- Confidently navigate on screen non-fiction texts.
- Use a range of questions to elicit relevant information.

If they need further support please refer to a prior Unit or a similar Unit in Year 4.

Resources

Photocopiable page 125 'Barrier games'; *How to make a moving toy 1* and *2* by Isabel Macdonald ❦ ; *Raspberry buns* by Jane Bower ❦; Photocopiable page 126 'Tips for writing great instructions'; Photocopiable page 127 'Create this!'; Photocopiable page 128 'How to make a'; Instruction skeleton ❦ Assessment activity 'Adventure playground rules' ❦

Cross-curricular opportunities

Design and technology
ICT

UNIT 1 ■ Teaching sequence

Phase	Children's objectives	Summary of activities	Learning outcomes
1	I can understand the difference between talk which may vary between formal and informal. I can compare the usefulness of techniques in giving instructions. I can punctuate sentences accurately. I can compare the usefulness of techniques in exploring the meaning of texts.	Give and follow instructions playing 'Barrier games'. Use instructions to guide a blindfolded partner around an obstacle course. Look at the punctuation of sentences, including commas. Give directions in the playground to direct a partner to find 'treasure'.	Children can use more formal aspects of language. Children can identify some of the difficulties that may arise if one or more communication modes are not available. Children can use more formal aspects of language.
2	I can compare different types of instruction text and identify how they are structured. I can adapt non-narrative forms and styles to write factual texts. I can reflect independently and critically on own writing and edit and improve it.	Deconstruct texts to identify language features of instructional texts. Create a picture on the computer using shapes and make notes of the instructions to give. Using notes, give instructions to a partner to create a picture on screen. Evaluate together the effectiveness of the instructions. Refine instructions in the light of feedback.	Children can identify key features of instructional texts and evaluate sets of instructions. Children can demonstrate that they can evaluate sets of instructions and attempt to follow some of them. Children can evaluate sets of instructions for layout, clarity and usefulness.
3	I can remember spelling strategies for spelling unstressed vowels. I can experiment with the order of sections and paragraphs. I can adapt sentence construction to different text types, purposes and readers. I can use a range of ICT programs to present texts. I can adapt sentence construction to different text-types, purposes and readers. I can use a range of ICT programs to present texts. I can reflect independently and critically on my own writing and edit and improve it.	Revise unstressed vowels. Use a skeleton to make notes for a set of instructions for something made in Design and technology. Shared writing. Draft first part of the instruction manual. Shared writing. Draft second part of instruction manual. Revise spellings. Refine a paragraph and improve it, ensuring accuracy.	Children can write an instructional text using appropriate form. Children can write an instructional text using appropriate form and features. Children can write an instructional text using appropriate form and features and awareness of intended audience. Children can reflect on their writing and edit and improve it.

Provide copies of the objectives for the children.

DAY 1 ▮ Barrier games

Key features	Stages	Additional opportunities

Enquiry: investigate a range of instructional texts

Communication: give and follow clear instructions

Empathy: imagine themselves in another person's position

Introduction
Tell the children that this Unit is about instructional texts. Explain that it is going to link to work they have done in ICT and design and technology. Discuss quickly some examples of different instructional texts (recipes, directions, how to make things, computer tutorials). Identify with the children the main purpose of instructional texts (to tell someone else how to do something). Explain that they are going to play some barrier games that involve pairs of them working together giving each other instructions on how to do something, but one partner cannot see what the other is doing. Model this for them using a table, some LEGO® pieces and a divider (barrier). Behind the barrier, you – the teacher – assemble the LEGO® into an object. You then give instructions to your partner so that they create the same object (make sure each person has the same pieces). Discuss with the children what you did to make the instructions clear.

Speaking and listening
Provide pairs of children with barriers and equipment, using photocopiable page 125 'Barrier games'. Ask them to play the game. Encourage the listeners to ask for clarification if they are not clear. Remove the barriers and discuss the results.

Plenary
Collect ideas from the children about what good instructions are. Record these on the board. Discuss the need for accurate instructions.

Support: provide the children with a selection of different connectives to join the instructions together, such as: *now, take, get, after that, next*

Extend: select more challenging games for the children to play

Support: provide clear rules using photocopiable page 125 'Barrier games'

DAY 2 ▮ Obstacle course

Key features	Stages	Additional opportunities

Empathy: imagine themselves in another person's position

Communication: give and follow clear instructions

Introduction
Recap with the children what they noticed from Day 1 about giving clear instructions. Explain that today they are going to create instructions for an obstacle course that pairs of children are going to do together. Tell them that while one member of the pair is giving the instructions, the other partner is going to be blindfolded so they will have to listen carefully. Prepare an obstacle course in the hall, using apparatus that will involve children walking over, under and through. Lay it out in lines so that four pairs of children can be working at once. Outline the course to the children and explain to them that their partner has to do all the challenges that they set. Model the activity with one child blindfolded. For example: *In front of you is a hoop. Step into it. Now bend down and pick up the hoop to your waist. Now swirl the hoop around so that it falls in circles to the ground.* Discuss with the children why it is important to say *in front of you* and so on, to orientate the listener.

Speaking and listening
Ask the children in their pairs (one blindfolded, one the instructor) to complete the obstacle course. When all the children have finished, discuss with them how clear the instructions were and what the listeners could do to improve. Swap roles and repeat.

Plenary
Identify with the children the importance of telling the listener what they are going to do. Being blindfolded, they need a very clear idea of what the task is.

Support: provide children with different positional words to enhance their vocabulary: *under, through, round, over, next to, in front, behind, left, right, backwards*

Extend: encourage the children to give more than one instruction at a time

Support: encourage the use of simple connectives and sequences of ideas in spoken instructions

DAY 3 ▪ Giving directions

Key features	Stages	Additional opportunities
Enquiry: investigate a range of instructional texts	### Introduction Write on the board the following two sentences: ■ *When you have completed the task, sit down on the floor.* ■ *Now take the spare card, the card you cut off earlier, and cut out the shape of a ball.* Explain that these sentences are giving instructions and that in order for them to be clear to the reader, they need to be punctuated properly. Discuss with the children the placement of the commas. In the first sentence, the comma separates a main clause from a dependent clause. In the second, the commas add in a phrase to clarify. Ask the children in pairs to write a few sentences that give directions, for example *walk ten steps forward, now turn right.* Ensure that they punctuate the sentences accurately using commas.	**Support**: remind children of mathematical language: *rotate through a right angle, walk diagonally* and so on
Communication: give and follow clear instructions		
Empathy: imagine themselves in another person's position	### Speaking and listening Take the children to the playground and explain that they need to direct their partners to some 'treasure' (bag of sweets, plastic coins and so on) while their partner is blindfolded. They can only use the instructions *left* and *right, forward* and *backward* and different angles. For example, *Walk forwards for ten large strides. Now stop and turn 90 degrees to the right.* Working in pairs, ask the children to take turns giving the instructions so that their partner gets to the treasure. Then ask the children to write some of the instructions they used and to punctuate them correctly, making use of commas.	**Extend:** ask the children to provide more complex sequences of instructions **Support:** let the children provide shorter instructions
	### Plenary Discuss with the children the success of different partnerships and why this was so. Invite them to read out their sentences and discuss punctuation.	

Guided reading
Use guided reading to read a wide range of different non-fiction genres. Encourage the children to evaluate the effectiveness of the layout and presentation in the text for:
■ clarity of conveying the facts
■ maintaining the interest of the reader
■ coherence of the language for the reader to understand.

Assessment
Informally assess children's vocabulary of positional language (*in, on, under, through* and so on).
Identify how well children vary the instructions they give so that they are not always using the same sentence sequence. Assess how well they modify the instructions for the different listeners.
Refer back to the learning outcomes on page 117.

Further work
Encourage the children to look for different examples of instructions from different sources, such as websites, newspapers, magazines and television.

DAY 1 ▪ The language features of instructional texts

Key features	Stages	Additional opportunities
Enquiry: investigate a range of instructional texts **Reasoning:** construct reasoned opinions **Information processing:** identify relevant information	### Introduction Remind the children that they have now given instructions orally to their partners in different contexts. Discuss what they would expect to see in instructions that were written down. List their ideas on the board. Provide them with copies of *How to make a moving toy Part 1* and *2* from the CD-ROM. Ask them, in pairs, to highlight the key features used from the list made on the board and to note by text-marking anything else that makes this an effective instructional text. Allow ten minutes for this activity and then take feedback, highlighting any language features that enhance the text. Emphasise the following: ■ tips that make things easier ■ phrases that help the reader be really clear about what they are doing ■ *This means that* – which provides a short explanation showing the reader why they are doing the activity. ### Independent work Provide the children with copies of the text *Raspberry buns* from the CD-ROM. Ask them to identify the language features using the list on the board as a starting point. ### Plenary Take feedback and add any extra features noticed to the list on the board.	**Support:** revise with the children different connectives used in instructional texts **Extend:** ask children to compare the two texts for effectiveness **Support:** provide children with photocopiable page 126 'Tips for writing great instructions'

DAY 2 ▪ How to create a picture using shapes

Key features	Stages	Additional opportunities
Information processing: use as a basis for written instructions **Communication:** give clear instructions **Evaluation:** judge effectiveness of their own work	### Introduction Explain to the children that this lesson links to work that they have done in ICT graphic modelling. Using a drawing tool bar, create a small graphic picture made up of shapes filled with different colours (see photocopiable page 127 'Create this!' for details). On a flipchart or in another window on the computer (tiled vertically), note down the order and icons used to create the picture. Explain that the children are going to write notes so that their partners can create the same pattern as them in the next lesson. As you write your notes as a model, remind the children of different strategies of note-taking (abbreviations, numbers, icons and key words/phrases). These notes are to act as memory triggers to them as they give the instructions in full sentences, so it is important that they know what they mean. ### Independent work Ask the children to individually create a picture using the drawing tool bar in a word-processing program. They then note down the order in which they created the shape, either in their books or on screen. Encourage the children to go through their notes to ensure that they have all the information, saying their instructions aloud and then creating the shape. Remind them to add in any additional notes that they may have missed. Print out copies of the shape that the children have drawn for reference in the next lesson. ### Plenary Ask the children to provide examples of their notes for writing instructions and to say them out loud, in full. Discuss the abbreviations they have made.	**Support:** provide the children with names of the icons on the drawing tool bar **Extend:** let children create their own patterns and make clear instructions **Support:** ask children to use photocopiable page 127 and follow the instructions to make the same pattern

DAY 3 ■ Were my instructions precise?

Key features	Stages	Additional opportunities
Evaluation: give feedback and judge effectiveness of their own work **Communication:** work collaboratively in pairs	**Introduction** Put the children into pairs. Ensure that each pair has access to a computer and that each child has the notes they made on how to make their shape together with a print-out of the shape. Explain that they are to give their partner instructions from their notes to create the shape on screen. Model the activity for them, asking one child to give you the instructions. Remind those who are drawing of the importance of clarifying what they have to do by asking questions: *What size should the shape be? Is it the outline that needs to be green or the whole shape?* Explain that these questions will tell the instructor which pieces of information they missed out; they will need to record this information in their notes. **Speaking and listening** Working in their pairs, ask the children to each give instructions for the other to draw their picture. When they have both finished, let them print the pictures and evaluate the instructions, discussing what needs to be put in to make them work even better. Repeat the activity so that each child has a further opportunity to refine their notes. **Plenary** Bring the lesson to a close by discussing the changes to the notes the children had to make. Highlight how important it is to imagine that the listener/reader has no knowledge of what you mean. Refer back to the barrier games and blindfolded games.	**Support:** reinforce good speaking and listening skills by defining the role of the speaker and the listener **Extend:** encourage children to create final versions of their instructions **Support:** provide a writing frame for children to record their instructions

Guided reading

Use guided reading to identify the features of different instructional texts. Compare:

■ differences in layout
■ use of instructional language
■ the degree to which short explanations are used for clarification
■ techniques for layout, including diagrams, labels, captions and so on, that aid understanding.

Assessment

Through observation and marking, informally assess the children's developing sense of the audience in their instructional writing.
Observe the children's ability to carry out instructions given.
Refer back to the learning outcomes on page 117.

Further work

Encourage the children to play a number of different barrier games using different subject matter to develop contextual vocabulary (particularly useful for EAL learners). For example, mathematical shapes and diagrams, creating maps on a grid and so on.

DAY 1 ▪ Planning the sections of the manual

Key features	Stages	Additional opportunities
Communication: reflect on different modes of communication

Information processing: identify relevant information and use this as a basis for written instructions | ### Introduction
Revise with the children the spelling of words with unstressed vowels through syllabification. Write the word *remember* on the board. Discuss the use of vowels in the word. Say that a way to remember how to spell a word is to syllabify it. Call out a number of other words, encouraging the children to remember to syllabify them in order to spell them, for example separate, prepare, easily, definite.

Display photocopiable page 128 'How to make a'. Explain to the children that they are going to write their own instruction manual for something they have made in design and technology (moving toys, biscuits, musical instruments). Model how to make simple notes to remember what they did when they made their item. Use an example of the outcome to trigger memories of what they did during the making process and record ideas on the board. Remind the children not to write in full sentences here, and discuss with them how to organise the different sections of the text. Keep a copy for later use. Also show the children the Instruction skeleton from the CD-ROM and how this can also help to plan writing instructions.

Independent work
Provide the children each with a copy of photocopiable page 128 'How to make a' and ask them to write their own notes for the sections.

Plenary
Encourage the children to use their notes from the photocopiable to tell a partner how to make their item. | recap other ways to remember spellings

Extend: let the children plan sections and paragraphs independently

Support: use a guided writing session to help the children plan the sequence of notes using the skeleton from the CD-ROM |

DAY 2 ▪ Drafting the manual

Key features	Stages	Additional opportunities
Communication: develop their ability to give clear instructions

Evaluation: judge the effectiveness of their own work

Information processing: identify relevant information and use this as a basis for written instructions | ### Introduction
Use shared writing to draft with the children the first part of their manual. Rehearse the written instructions orally. Refer back, to your copy of photocopiable page 128 from Day 1. Write down the equipment needed and record this using a layout of your choice, such as bullet points. If necessary, divide the equipment into two sections, essential equipment and added extras and decoration. Discuss together the first instruction. Take a few examples and ask the children to refine these into the most precise instructions they can. If necessary, model how to do this. Record a well refined sentence on the board and discuss what will logically come next to extend and expand the idea. Read back two or three sentences to be sure that the writing is as precise as it could be. Discuss different phrases used to make it really clear, for example *make sure that..., do this so that...* and so on.

Independent work
Ask the children to draft their writing for the first half of their manual, either onto a word processor or by hand. Provide guided writing for specific groups.

Plenary
Ask the children to read out what they consider to be their best written instruction, explaining their thinking. | remind children of the importance of punctuation

Extend: allow children to lay out their own text, using their own modifications

Support: provide connectives as starters for writing, for example: *Next, get the..., You need this so ...* |

DAY 3 ■ Drafting the second part of the manual

Key features	Stages	Additional opportunities
.Communication: develop their ability to give instructions Evaluation: give feedback and judge effectiveness of their own work	**Introduction** Ask the children to feed back to you the purpose and audience of their writing. Discuss how they may need to modify their writing with their audience in mind. Explain that they are going to complete their writing today. Return to the file or text that you modelled yesterday. Recap on the writing and read it through. Explain why this is important for the children to do when they return to their own texts. Using shared writing, write the next section of the instructions. Discuss the instructions and take feedback from the children, listening to a number of examples. Ask them to listen for instructional language, such as imperative verbs, as well as clear detail. Encourage them to identify what may have been left out and refine the instructions orally. Record a series of sentences on the board making sure that each sentence starts a different way, read them back and discuss the vocabulary use, the connectives and punctuation. Are they clear enough? Repeat for another point. Keep a copy. **Independent work** Ask the children to complete the second half of their writing. **Plenary** Encourage the children to read their instructions to a partner. Have they included everything?	**Extend:** children write their instructions clearly, using different ways to start each sentence **Support:** provide a simple frame for the second part of the writing

DAY 4 ■ Is the manual clear enough?

Key features	Stages	Additional opportunities
	Introduction Write a number of words on the board, for example *difference, frightening, familiar, deafening, different, Wednesday, miserable.* Use one word as a model and discuss the different ways of remembering its unstressed vowel: root word, building up the prefix and the suffix, saying the word as it might sound and syllabification. Ask the children to come up with strategies for remembering at least four of the words. Using whiteboards, say a word out loud and ask the children to write it down. Provide a correct model for them to check against. Encourage them to use the strategies they identified. Display a paragraph from the shared writing activity on Day 3. Explain that as a class they are going to look critically at the paragraph to see if there are any improvements to be made. Remind the children of the tips for good instructional texts. Ask the children for suggestions for improvements. Modify the enlarged text with them and then create a redrafted paragraph.	**Extend:** the children revise all their manual paragraph by paragraph
Evaluation: discuss success criteria, give feedback and judge the effectiveness of their own work	**Independent work** Ask the children to choose one of their paragraphs to work on. Encourage them to identify omissions in instructions they have made, and then add these in to develop and extend the paragraph by rewriting it. **Plenary** Ask the children to compare old and new versions and identify improvements.	**Support:** provide children with equipment to make the item using instructions and correcting them accordingly

Guided reading

Encourage the children to read a range of web based material to become familiar with how to navigate the text on screen and how to make notes and gain information.

Discuss the layout with the children, including the use of hyperlinks as a means of guiding the reader efficiently to the information they want.

Identify also where web pages are overcrowded and difficult to navigate and identify reasons why, such as lack of clarity, inappropriate font size and so on.

Assessment

Formally assess the children's understanding of instructional writing by using the assessment sheet 'Adventure playground rules' from the CD-ROM.

From the children's own writing, identify key areas of instructional writing they are weaker on, as well as generic aspects of writing, such as: punctuation, control over writing more complex sentences and so on.

Refer back to the learning outcomes on page 117.

Further work

Ask the children create a final version of their manuals to display with their Design and technology models.

Barrier games

Rules for Barrier games

■ Two players are sitting opposite one another with a barrier in between them.

■ One child gives a set of instructions to their partner so that they draw/create the same picture/model.

■ The listener may ask questions for clarification.

■ The speaker needs to make the instructions as clear as possible to the listener.

■ When the speaker has said all the instructions the barrier is removed and the children check that they have the same picture/model.

Different ways to play

■ Draw patterns on your page using 2D shapes. Make sure your partner has the same shapes.

■ Create shapes using building bricks. Make sure your partner has the same building bricks.

■ Use squared paper and felt-tipped pens to draw a pattern. Make sure you tell your partner exactly which square and the colour it should be.

■ Draw an x and y axis. Draw a shape on the axis and give your partner the coordinates. Make sure you always give the x coordinate first.

Tips for writing great instructions

■ Make sure you are really clear about the order that things happen in.

■ Use a variety of different connectives to join your ideas and your sentences together. Try not to use 'then' too much.

■ Remember that your audience will not know what to do so add a diagram if necessary.

■ Add an extra bit of explanation to tell the reader why they are doing it. These connectives are useful 'This is because…' or 'Make sure that…'

■ Include a tip to tell the reader how to do it more easily.

■ Include technical language as far as you can so that your writing is precise.

■ Use bullet points, or numbers to help make the writing clear.

■ Give a clear title to show exactly what the instructions are for.

Create this!

Follow these instructions to create this picture.

■ Click on the rectangle on the drawing toolbar and draw a rectangle to fill the page. Click on the fill colour icon and choose blue.

■ Click on the autoshapes button, go to stars and banners and choose a banner. Then on the page and click and drag the cursor on the coloured square.

■ Make sure the banner is highlighted so that you can use the fill colour icon to make the banner a yellow colour. You should now have one shape on the background rectangle.

■ Return to the autoshapes button on the drawing toolbar and go to basic shapes to find the triangle, pentagon and rectangle. Place these on the blue backgound. Return to stars and banners to find the jagged shape and star.

■ Place each of the shapes in the same places on the rectangular background as they are on the picture above and fill them so they are the same colours.

■ To put one shape behind the other, highlight the shape which you want to go behind another by clicking on it. Right-click your mouse when the cursor is over the highlighted shape and highlight order. Click on 'send to back' to put the shapes one behind the other.

■ Do this for all the shapes needed.

NON-FICTION ■ UNIT 1

How to make a

What you will need:

_____

_____

_____

_____

_____

_____

Stage 1

■ _____

■ _____

■ _____

Stage 2

■ _____

■ _____

■ _____

Stage 3

■ _____

■ _____

■ _____

Useful tips

_____

_____

NON-FICTION
UNIT 2 Reports and explanations

Speak and listen for a range of purposes on paper and on screen

Strand 1 Speaking
- Use and explore different question types and different ways words are used, including formal and informal contexts.

Strand 2 Listening and responding
- Identify different question types and evaluate their impact on the audience.
- Identify some different aspects of talk that vary between formal and informal occasions.

Strand 3 Group discussion and interaction
- Plan and manage a group task over time using different levels of planning.
- Understand different ways to take the lead and support others in groups.
- Understand the process of decision making.

Strand 4 Drama
- Reflect on how working in role helps to explore complex issues.

Read for a range of purposes on paper and on screen

Strand 6 Word structure and spelling
- Know and use less common prefixes and suffixes such as *im-, ir-, -cian.*
- Group and classify words according to their spelling patterns and their meanings.

Strand 7 Understanding and interpreting texts
- Make notes on and use evidence from across a text to explain events or ideas.
- Compare different types of narrative and information texts and identify how they are structured.

Strand 8 Engaging with and responding to texts
- Reflect on reading habits and preferences and plan personal reading goals.

Write for a range of purposes on paper and on screen

Strand 9 Creating and shaping texts
- Reflect independently and critically on their own writing and edit and improve it.
- Adapt non-narrative forms and styles to write fiction or factual texts, including poems.
- Create multi-layered texts, including use of hyperlinks and web pages.

Strand 10 Text structure and organisation
- Experiment with the order of sections and paragraphs to achieve different effects.
- Change the order of material within a paragraph, moving the topic sentence.

Strand 11 Sentence structure and punctuation
- Adapt sentence construction to different text-types, purposes and readers.
- Punctuate sentences accurately, including using speech marks and apostrophes.

Strand 12 Presentation
- Adapt handwriting for specific purposes, for example printing, use of italic.
- Use a range of ICT programs to present texts, making informed choices about which electronic tools to use for different purposes.

Progression in reports and explanations

In this year, children are moving towards:
- Collecting information to write a report in which two or more subjects are compared; solids, liquids and gases, observing that a grid rather than a

▶

spidergram is appropriate for representing the information.
■ Drawing attention to the precision in the use of technical terminology and how many of the nouns are derived from verbs.
■ Engaging in teacher demonstration of the writing of a non-chronological report, including the use of organisational devices to aid conciseness.
■ Planning, composing, editing and refining short non-chronological comparative report, focusing on clarity, conciseness and impersonal style.
■ Reading and analysing a range of explanatory texts, investigating and noting features of impersonal style.
■ Engaging in teacher demonstration of how to research and plan a page for a reference book on one aspect of a class topic using shared note-making and writing of the page, using an impersonal style, hypothetical language and causal and temporal connections as appropriate.

Key aspects of learning covered in this Unit

Enquiry
Children will seek, interpret and use the answers to their own questions as well as those of others in their activity throughout this Unit.

Information processing
Children will know where to find information and understand what is relevant and locate this within sources. They will use strategies such as scanning, skimming and using an index to locate information. They will identify the most relevant information from different sources and use this as a basis for writing.

Evaluation
Children will compare and evaluate the effectiveness of recount texts in a variety of forms. They will share their own writing outcomes, discuss success criteria, give feedback to others and judge the effectiveness of their own work.

Communication
They will develop their ability to discuss effective and relevant communication in respect of both the form and the content of the non-fiction texts they read or access and write or create. They will often work collaboratively in pairs or groups. They will communicate outcomes orally and in writing.

Prior learning

Before starting this Unit check that the children can:
■ Recall the language features and organisation of recount texts and reports.
■ Use a range of questions to elicit relevant information.
■ Understand the difference between direct and reported speech.
If they need further support please refer to a prior Unit or a similar Unit in Year 4.

Resources

The Sun by Campbell Perry ❄; *Water Cycle* by Bender Richardson White ❄; Recount skeketon ❄; Photocopiable page 141 'Making notes from information texts'; Photocopiable page 142 'Effective note-taking strategies'; Photocopiable page 143 'Writing a paragraph'; Photocopiable page 144 'Criteria for writing a developed paragraph'; Assessment activity 'Sorting statements' ❄

Cross-curricular opportunities

Science
ICT
History

UNIT 2 ■ Teaching sequence

Phase	Children's objectives	Summary of activities	Learning outcomes
1	I can identify features of recount texts, recognising how they are structured. I can use and explore different question types and different ways words are used, including formal and informal contexts.	Make notes from a website about a famous person. Identify different question types and practise interviewing techniques.	Children can recognise the features of recounts in different texts. Children can demonstrate an understanding of the most effective questioning techniques.
2	I can adapt non-narrative forms and styles to write fiction and factual texts. I can make notes on and use evidence from across a text to explain events or ideas. I can make notes on and use evidence from across a text to explain events or ideas. I can experiment with the order of sections and paragraphs to achieve different effects.	Write a biographical recount using notes made previously. Develop understanding of reports and make notes. Research a number of sources to find information and make notes. Use notes to write two versions of the same paragraph.	Children can identify the features of the most successful recount texts. Children can make notes from a given text. Children can research from more than one source and make notes. Children can write in paragraphs appropriately and use connections well.
3	I can create multi-layered texts including use of hyperlinks. I can compare different types of information texts and identify how they are structured. I can practise use of cause and effect language. I can use a range of ICT programs to present texts, making informed choices about which electronic tools to use for different purposes. I can use less common suffixes. I can understand the order of paragraphs to improve writing. I can know and use less common prefixes and suffixes. I can reflect independently and critically on own writing and edit it. I can group and classify words according to their spelling patterns and their meanings.	Create multimedia presentation texts from information researched. Analyse the effectiveness of and differences between report and explanation texts. Identify cause and effect language for writing good explanations. Using a computer, create a visual diagram for an explanation text. Learn suffixes. Identify the features of a good paragraph and practise writing their own. Revise prefixes. Improve the effectiveness of the explanation text through discussion, shared writing and working on own texts. Learn strategies to remember homophones and homonyms and practise spellings for different words.	Children can create a multimedia presentation of their work. Children can understand the differences between report and explanation texts. Children can construct sentences using cause and effect language. Children can create a diagram with labels to illustrate an explanation text. Children can write and order paragraphs for an explanation text. Children can refine, edit and improve their writing following agreed criteria. Children can identify strategies for remembering homophones and homonyms and can spell words correctly.

Provide copies of the objectives for the children.

DAY 1 ▰ What is a recount?

Key features	Stages	Additional opportunities
Enquiry: seek, interpret and use the answers to their own questions as well as those of others	**Introduction** This lesson can be used to study any relevant famous person, for example a musician, politician or a famous writer. Explain to the children that the Unit is going to cover three different text types that they should be familiar with: recounts, explanations and reports. Using a flipchart to record suggestions, discuss with them the features of a recount. Remind them of the purpose (to retell events in sequential order, to inform an unknown reader). As a class choose a famous person and look at a website of their life. Through shared reading, ask the children to identify the features of a recount (events in order, past tense and so on). Use the Recount skeleton from the CD-ROM to record the examples of these features and to make notes about this person's life. (Keep a copy.) **Independent work** Provide the children with a printed version of the website text and a copy of the Recount skeleton from the CD-ROM. Ask them to identify and summarise the main ideas and facts of each paragraph to put in note form onto their skeleton. Keep copies of their work.	**Extend:** discuss the different types of text that could be recounts (biography, autobiography, sports match reports) **Extend:** ask children to read each paragraph and summarise the main idea beside it **Support:** let children summarise fewer paragraphs, underlining key information to identify the main ideas
Information processing: identify the most relevant information	**Plenary** As a class, go through each paragraph of the website text identifying the main idea in each one.	

DAY 2 ▰ Using different question types

Key features	Stages	Additional opportunities
Speaking: use and explore different question types and ways words are used, including formal and informal contexts	**Introduction** Explain to the children that they are going to 'interview' the chosen famous person. Discuss different types of questions that they could use (open, closed, probing, follow up). Ask them to write down four different types of questions that link to the person's life. Discuss how they might approach the interview. If they knew the famous person personally, how would they address them? Discuss ways that they might phrase the questions to indicate that they are less familiar with them. Record a few question starters on the board that highlight the difference between formal and more familiar questioning. **Speaking and listening** Choose a child to take on the role of the famous person. The others take turns to ask questions and listen to the responses. Discuss with the children how they could have rephrased the questions and perhaps had a different response.	**Support:** remind the children of different ways of starting questions **Extend:** ensure that the children use a range of question types
Communication: discuss effective communication **Evaluation:** judge effectiveness of their own work	**Independent work** In pairs, the children plan questions and then role play interviewing each other. **Plenary** Ask a group of children to show their paired interviews. Provide the listeners with four 'show me' cards labelled *open, closed, probing* and *follow up*. As the interview proceeds, ask the children to show, by raising the relevant card, which kind of question was used at each point. Discuss the responses.	**Support:** provide different question stems to support the planning of questions: *How did you...?*

Guided reading

Use a variety of non-fiction texts to read with the children, discussing effective ways to retrieve information using skimming and scanning techniques as well as a focused read.

Assessment

Through observation during whole-class and paired work, assess the children's ability to ask different questions to elicit high quality information.

Refer back to the learning outcomes on page 131.

Further work

Use a number of different types of recount texts, encouraging the children to identify the similar features, for example: biography, autobiography, sports reports.

DAY 1 ◼ Biographical writing

Key features	Stages	Additional opportunities
Information processing: identify the most relevant information as a basis for writing **Evaluation:** give feedback and judge effectiveness of their own work	**Introduction** Remind the children of the work completed on Day 1 of Phase 1 and refer back to the notes made together. Show the children how to write the key events of the person's life chronologically. Point out that there needs to be a balance of factual events, such as dates, times and places, as well as evidence of the person's interests, likes and dislikes. Model for the children how to turn notes into a short piece of writing about the person's life. Explain that you are only going to model the beginning of the text, which is the introduction and that it needs to tell the reader who the person was, why they were famous and for what they will be remembered. **Independent work** Referring to the notes made on Day 1 of Phase 1, ask the children to write their own recount of the famous person's life. They can use the shared writing as a starting point and then continue working independently. **Plenary** Ask the children quickly to identify the best phrase or sentence they have written that sounds the most literary. Discuss briefly what has made it so, for example, the use of facts, the sentence construction (including the use of connectives) and so on.	**Support:** remind children of the different connectives used in recount texts **Extend:** get the children to use a wider range of connectives – not just *then* **Support:** provide a frame with key connectives to structure the paragraphs

DAY 2 ◼ Making notes from information texts

Key features	Stages	Additional opportunities
Enquiry: seek, interpret and use the answers to their own questions **Communication:** discuss effective and relevant communication **Information processing:** understand what is relevant and locate this within the sources	**Introduction** This lesson links to Science but can be adapted to suit other curriculum areas. Explain to the children that they are going to be looking at how to make notes from texts to explain ideas. Using an enlarged version of photocopiable page 141 'Making notes from information texts', discuss with the children what they already know about the Sun. Record their knowledge in the relevant column. Discuss and generate questions that they would like to find out about the Sun. Record these. Tell them that one text may not provide all the information to answer these questions. Show them the text *The Sun* from the CD-ROM and model how to navigate the text by skimming to get a sense of what it is about. Refer back to the questions recorded and use the key words in the questions to focus the scanning of the text to find the answers. Ensure that, in the questions you model, you include one or two to which you know the answers are definitely in the text, for example: *What is a sun spot? What is the Sun made up of?* Model for the children how to take notes by identifying the key words and phrases in the text that answer the question. **Independent work** Provide the children with copies of *The Sun* from the CD-ROM and photocopiable page 141 'Making notes from information texts'. Ask them to make notes by text-marking, identifying key words from the text. **Plenary** Discuss with the children how to home in on key words – identify what to include and what to leave out. Remind them that it is important to maintain sense in the notes. Ask them to use their notes to explain what they know about the Sun.	**Support:** remind the children of ways to delete words that are not relevant and how to record notes **Extend:** encourage the children to summarise the main ideas prior to making notes **Support:** provide the children with two or three key questions and short paragraphs from the text *The Sun* where the answers are

DAY 3 ■ Make notes from other sources

Key features	Stages	Additional opportunities
Enquiry: seek, interpret and use the answers to their own questions **Communication:** work collaboratively in pairs **Information processing:** use strategies such as scanning, skimming and using an index to locate information	### Introduction Explain to the children that they are going to use different sources to research information about the Solar System. Provide them with a number of relevant reference texts as well as the following website: http://www.icteachers.co.uk/children/cyberhunts/solar_system/sosystem.htm. Model for the children how to create their own notes using their own words. Show them how to structure their note-taking by creating a small grid with key questions similar to photocopiable page 141 'Making notes from information texts'. Remind them that the text can only answer some questions. Refine their searches to a few key questions. Explain that if they do not find the answers to these questions but find interesting information along the way, they can record that too. Go to the website mentioned above and show the children how to find information and then interpret it by rephrasing it in their heads or out loud before writing it down, for example: *The planet is covered in thick cloud* can become *Surface covered in cloud*. Discuss whether the note made has changed the meaning of the text sentence or the fact. (Keep a copy.) ### Independent work Ask the children to research the planets of their choice and make notes using a variety of sources. Give them copies of photocopiable page 142 'Effective note-taking strategies' to help them. (Keep copies of their work.) ### Plenary Encourage the children to explain to a partner the facts they have found out. When there is confusion, ask them to refer back to the original source to clarify.	**Extend:** provide the children with more than one type of source material, encouraging them to cross reference **Support:** direct the children to a specific planet and provide them with prepared questions to answer

DAY 4 ■ Writing a paragraph of details

Key features	Stages	Additional opportunities
Information processing: identify relevant information and use this as a basis for writing **Communication:** discuss effective and relevant communication	### Introduction Return to the notes made yesterday about the planets. Say that, in this lesson, the children are going to put these notes into complete sentences to create a paragraph of information about one of the planets they have researched. Explain that the lesson will focus on the most effective order of the sentences within the paragraph for the reader. Using the notes you made in the previous lesson, model through shared writing how to turn these into a paragraph of writing. Write two versions of the same paragraph, showing the children how ordering the information in different ways can create a different effect for the reader. (Keep a copy.) ### Independent work Using their notes from the previous lesson, ask the children to write two versions of the same paragraph by putting the information in a different order Use photocopiable page 143 'Writing a paragraph' as a frame to support the structure of the paragraph. Encourage them to use a number of different ways of joining their sentences together so that they are not always using *then*. ### Plenary Ask the children to identify which paragraph they think is the more effective at informing the reader clearly about the information they have researched. Create a list of key points for writing an effective paragraph with them.	**Support:** remind the children of the key features of report texts: present tense and inclusion of technical vocabulary **Extend:** use photocopiable page 143 to explore writing two different paragraphs **Support:** modify photocopiable page 143 to include specific connectives to support writing

Guided reading

Read a range of different non-fiction texts with the children, supporting them to use the features of reports and explanations, such as headings, bullet points and captions to aid the techniques of skimming and scanning.

Teach the children to summarise orally the information they have found by paraphrasing and using their own words.

Assessment

Provide the children with three examples of different paragraphs they have written and ask them to identify the one that they think is the best. Ask them to explain why it is better than the others and then create some criteria for assessing, which they can use to assess their own paragraphs. Refer back to the learning outcomes on page 131.

Further work

Provide the children with further opportunities to make notes using other curriculum areas as subject matter. Alternatively, teach them to apply the skills they have learned by making notes in another curriculum area.

DAY 1 ■ Creating a multimedia presentation

Key features	Stages	Additional opportunities
Information processing: identify relevant information from different sources	**Introduction** It is a good idea to do this lesson in an ICT suite. Explain to the children that they are going to create their own multimedia presentation to display the information about their planet from Days 3 and 4. Using the paragraph that you modelled in the previous lesson as a starting point, show the children how to create a presentation by using a multimedia package. Explain how to insert hyperlinks to key words that you have used in your text. Insert a number of relevant pictures to the work and show the children how to create labels and diagrams to explain what you mean. Show the children how they can use the presentation to explain about the planet to an audience by giving a talk.	
Communication: work collaboratively in pairs	**Independent work** Using their notes and paragraphs and working in pairs, ask the children to create their own multimedia presentations about the planets of their choice. Once their presentations are complete, ask them to rehearse orally, using the presentation as a tool to explain visually the information about their planet.	**Extend:** let children use the custom animation tool on a presentation package to create information
Evaluation: discuss success criteria and give feedback to others	**Plenary** Select groups of children to present their researched information. Ask the class to evaluate the presentations for their clarity of information sharing, explanation of technical words and so on.	**Support:** ask children to incorporate simple facts from their research

DAY 2 ■ Compare different types of information texts

Key features	Stages	Additional opportunities
	Introduction Display the texts *The Sun* and *Water Cycle* from the CD-ROM. Through shared reading, identify the purpose of each text with the children. Discuss both the similarities and differences between the texts. Focus on the following areas: layout, paragraphing, features, labels, use of illustrations and vocabulary. Discuss with the children how the writing is different. Read a paragraph from each of the texts and ask them to identify the key language features used. ■ Report text: present tense, technical vocabulary, key facts ■ Explanation text: present tense, facts, cause and effect sentences (connectives such as *when* or *as*), diagrams.	**Extend:** give the children copies of a number of different texts that are either explanations or reports and ask them to sort them by identifying their language features
Enquiry: compare recount texts in a variety of forms	Explain to the children that there are subtle differences between the texts which are to do with their separate purposes. Remind them that one is to explain a process, the other to tell how things are.	**Extend:** let children create their own list of features for both genres
Information processing: understand what is relevant and locate information	**Independent work** Provide the children with a paragraph from each text and ask them to identify which is the explanation and which the report by identifying the language features as described above. Tell them to text-mark each feature.	**Support:** provide children with copies of a paragraph from each text, chopped up, to sort and order
	Plenary Take feedback from different groups and record their comments.	

DAY 3 ◗ Cause and effect language

Key features	Stages	Additional opportunities
Communication: discuss effective and relevant communication	### Introduction Explain to the children that they are going to look at how sentences in explanation texts have a cause and effect. Link this lesson to work in science. Discuss with children the different effects that happened in the experiments of evaporation and condensation. Create the following visual concept on a board:  In each of the circles record simple causes and effects, such as: *Kettle boiled – steam came out*, or *temperature changed – air condensed*. For each simple statement, identify which part was the cause and which the effect. Using the following conjunctions – *when, as, because, this means that, so* – experiment with creating sentences that show a cause and effect: *When the kettle boiled, the water turned to steam. This means that the water has evaporated, turning into steam because it reached boiling point.* Discuss how the second sentence expands on the first and clarifies it. ### Independent work Provide the children with other statements from *Water Cycle* from the CD-ROM that they can explain using the same technique, the second sentence clarifying the first. ### Plenary Take feedback from some of the children, refining and clarifying their writing.	**Extend:** discuss the punctuation of complex sentences with the children **Extend:** provide the children with specific conjunctions to use: *when, as, because, this means that* **Support:** use simpler conjunctions: *because, when, so* and relate to familiar experiences such as *The children behaved well, so they went out to play*

DAY 4 ◗ Creating a diagram for an explanation text

Key features	Stages	Additional opportunities
Information processing: know where to find information and understand what is relevant	### Introduction Use the ICT suite for this lesson and refer to *Water Cycle* from the CD-ROM. Explain to the children that they are going to use a word-processing program to draw and label their own explanation text of the water cycle. Identify the potential audience for this text and discuss the level of detail needed in the captions. Explain that they are going to write the main body of the text later but the diagram must provide a clear image to aid the reader's understanding and they must think carefully about the shapes they use in their diagrams. (Keep a copy.)	**ICT:** revise with the children the use of the drawing toolbar to create diagrams; remind them of the skills taught in graphic modelling **Extend:** encourage the use of text boxes to label and provide explanations
Communication: work collaboratively in pairs	### Independent work Ask the children, working either in pairs or individually, to use their scientific knowledge to create a diagram of the water cycle. They are applying the skills learned in one curriculum area to another. (Keep copies of their work.) ### Plenary At the end of the lesson, show a number of different examples of the children's work and discuss the effectiveness of the diagrams. What things are really clear, what things are less clear? Identify areas that need improving.	**Support:** provide simple instructions to support ideas of symbols and shapes to choose from

DAY 5 ▪ Understand the order of paragraphs

Key features	Stages	Additional opportunities

Communication: discuss effective and relevant communication

Introduction

Provide the children with a number of different suffixes, for example: -cian as in magician, -sion as in collision, -ssion as in possession, -tion as in fraction, -ition as in competition. Ask them briefly to think of other words with the same suffixes and record these on their whiteboards. Discuss how the words can be remembered by thinking about the preceding vowel.

Go back to the diagrams of the water cycle created yesterday. Discuss the possible aspects of the water cycle that need to be written into the text as separate paragraphs, such as: an introductory paragraph explaining the context; explanation of condensation, evaporation and so on. Discuss with the children the key aspects that make a good paragraph. Provide copies of photocopiable page 144 'Criteria for writing a developed paragraph' and ask the children to identify the features of a good paragraph in the text. Using an enlarged version, highlight the key areas of the text. Using shared writing, draft a subsequent paragraph headed *Evaporation in the water cycle* with the children. As you write, discuss what information needs to come next.

Extend: children to write a set of paragraphs

Support: let children write one paragraph ensuring the use of cause and effect connectives

Further work: ask children to redraft their paragraphs and insert them into their word-processed files using text boxes creating a complete page about the water cycle

Independent work

Ask the children to write their own paragraphs to go with their diagrams from Day 4. Discuss the order and placement of the paragraphs and how they will enhance the diagram. (Keep copies of their work.)

Evaluation: judge the effectiveness of their own work

Plenary

Encourage the children to evaluate the effectiveness of their written paragraphs by using the criteria outlined on photocopiable page 144.

DAY 6 ▪ Reviewing my work

Key features	Stages	Additional opportunities

Communication: discuss effective and relevant communication

Introduction

Provide the children with individual whiteboards and pens. Play 'Flash spelling' with them focusing on words that have less common suffixes such as: *distribution, pollution, revolution, extension, collision, nation, station.* Identify with the children the different vowel sounds that come before the *shun* sound. Give the root word for some of the words, for example: *extend, collide, exclude, delete* and so on and ask them to add on the *shun* sound choosing the suffix to put on.

Using an example of the children's writing from the previous lesson, discuss with them the effectiveness of the explanation in clarifying the exact process to someone who knows nothing about it. Ask the children to evaluate and improve the writing using the following criteria:

■ *Does the reader have a clear idea of the effects of evaporation, condensation and so on?*
■ *Does the text explain clearly how these effects create the water cycle?*
■ *Does the text define for the reader what the water cycle is?*
■ *Has the writer used enough technical language and accurate information?*

Support: remind the children of strategies to spell longer polysyllabic words (by syllabification)

Extend: let children revise their work in pairs, following the criteria

Evaluation: discuss success criteria

Independent work

Working in pairs, ask the children to read each other's texts and provide critical improvements. They then refine their own texts.

Support: use guided writing to review the children's writing

Evaluation: judge the effectiveness of their own work

Plenary

Encourage the children to explain their editing and improvements.

DAY 7 ■ Homophones and homonyms

Key features	Stages	Additional opportunities
Communication: communicate outcomes orally and in writing	**Introduction** Provide the children with a number of pairs of spellings of the same words, such as: *sell, cell; rein, rain, reign; rode, road, rowed; two, to, too; cent, scent, sent; there, they're, their*. Discuss which is the correct spelling with the children by providing the context of the word. For example, say a sentence and ask the children to write down the correct spelling of the word related to its meaning: *The man rowed his boat along the river.* *The man rode his horse.* *The man walked down the road.* Each context provides the spelling pattern. Discuss with children ways of remembering the different spellings and their contexts. Repeat for other ways of spelling. **Independent work** Provide the children with an number of homophones, in particular the following: *sew, so, sow; by, buy, bye*. Ask the children to write a sentence using the correct context and spelling pattern. **Plenary** Devise a number of visual strategies such as pictures and mnemonics/rhymes, to help the children remember the different contexts for the correct spelling of these words.	**Further work:** revise some of the long vowel phonemes that have spelling patterns but different pronunciations: *ough, our, ear, ie, oo* **Extend:** use dictionaries to find out meanings in context **Support:** let children practise strategies to remember common words they misspell

Guided reading

Read a range of non-fiction texts with the children, focusing on the following areas:
■ Structure and layout of the text
■ How the writer explains, informs, tells, instructs or persuades the reader effectively
■ How paragraphs are structured to develop an idea and add detail.

Assessment

Assess the children's understanding of the structure and language features of different text-types from their written work and learning outcomes (for example: the ICT explanation text of the water cycle; the recount of the famous person and the multimedia report). Use the assessment task 'Sorting statements' from the CD-ROM to support this. You can also use these outcomes to assess the children's application of ICT skills in another subject area. Refer back to the learning outcomes on page 131.

Further work

Expand and develop the children's ability to structure explanation texts by identifying other processes in other curriculum areas they could explain, for example: the differences between solids, liquids and gases.

Making notes from information texts

■ Fill in all three columns below about a chosen topic.

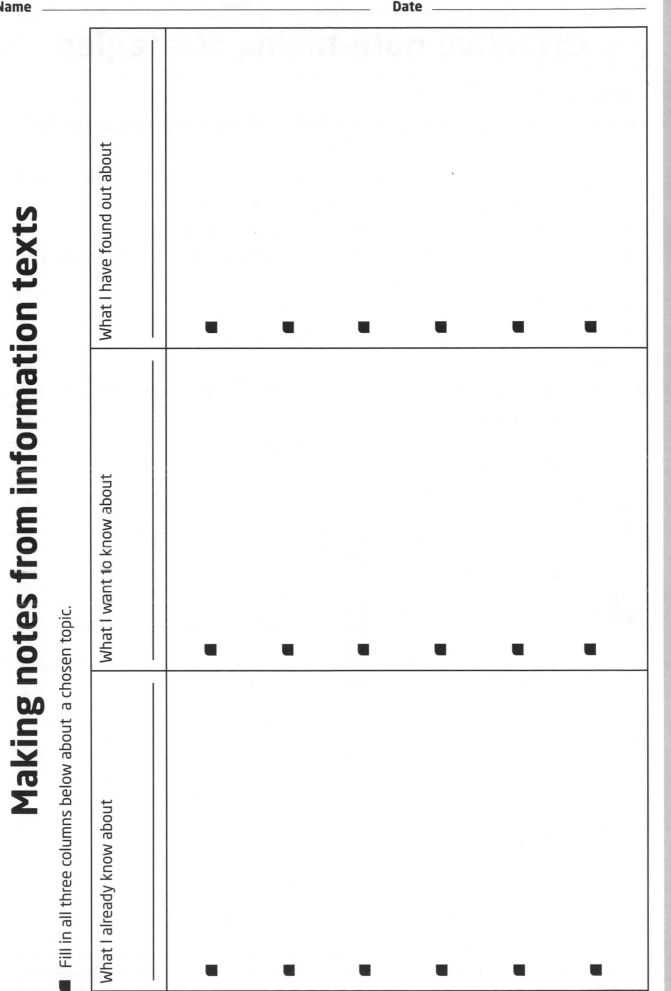

What I already know about	What I want to know about	What I have found out about
■	■	■
■	■	■
■	■	■
■	■	■
■	■	■
■	■	■

Effective note-taking strategies

Always try to...

■ Be clear about what you are finding out about – write down some key questions to which you want answers to.

■ Locate the information by skimming a page to see if the information you want is there – be clear what kinds of words or phrases you are looking for.

■ Use an index or chapter heading to decide if the source is relevant.

■ When you find the information you want, read the whole sentence or paragraph to be sure you have the right information.

■ Highlight key words and phrases which are relevant.

■ Rephrase the answer in your own words and write it down.

■ Choose a paragraph from a book to find out information. Choose a note-taking strategy to use to make notes below.

Note-taking criteria I used	Notes that I made from reading
■ ■ ■	_____ _____ _____

The note-taking strategy that was most helpful to me was

_____

It was helpful because _____

_____

PHOTOCOPIABLE
www.scholastic.co.uk

Writing a paragraph

■ Use this frame to write a clear paragraph that gives details to the reader about the planet you are writing about. Use the notes you made to help you.

Title or subheading

_____

Step 1

General statement that tells the reader what the paragraph is going to be about.

_____
_____
_____

Step 2

A sentence that explains or expands on one fact about the topic you have introduced.

_____
_____

Step 3

Three different facts about the planet that are of interest to the reader. Explain any unknown terms to them so the reader understands.
You can put these three facts in any order.

_____
_____
_____
_____

Criteria for writing a developed paragraph

■ Read the checklist for writing a good paragraph and then identify the techniques used in the paragraph below. Identify features by drawing a line to them.

- ■ Start with a general sentence that tells the reader what the paragraph is going to talk about.
- ■ Develop the idea by providing more information about one thing.
- ■ Provide the reader with a range of useful facts and information about the subject you are talking about.
- ■ Anything you think the reader will not know about explain in more detail using connectives such as: this means that, as a result, when this happens...
- ■ Try not to start each sentence the same way or with the same connectives - limit the times you use 'then'.
- ■ Don't repeat words find an alternative.

Facts and information   General opening statement

Connectives used   More information

Different words that mean the same thing   Different sentence starters

The water cycle

What is the water cycle?

The water cycle is the process by which water is recycled by nature so that it can be used again. Water is able to be used again because it exists in three different states: solid (as ice), liquid (as water) and gas (as water vapour). Water moves around our planet in these three different states. It is through the processes of evaporation and condensation that it changes its state. For example, water exists in the air because it evaporates from its liquid form to become a gas or water vapour. Clouds are made of water vapour, when you look at them in the sky you are actually looking at water stored as a gas. Another example is when water in a puddle disappears because the Sun has come out. The liquid water has turned into water vapour because the heat from the Sun has caused it to change state. As the temperature changes, water stored as a gas in clouds condenses and we get rainfall. The rain falls onto the land and the process continues in a cycle as evaporation will occur again.

NON-FICTION
UNIT 3 Persuasive writing

Speak and listen for a range of purposes on paper and on screen

Strand 1 Speaking
- Present a spoken argument, sequencing points logically, defending views with evidence and making use of persuasive language.

Strand 2 Listening and responding
- Identify some different aspects of talk that vary between formal and informal occasions.
- Analyse the use of persuasive language.

Strand 3 Group discussion and interaction
- Understand different ways to take the lead and support others in groups.
- Understand the process of decision making.

Strand 4 Drama
- Reflect on how working in role helps to explore complex issues.

Read for a range of purposes on paper and on screen

Strand 7 Understanding and interpreting texts
- Make notes on and use evidence from across a text to explain events or ideas.
- Infer writer's perspectives from what is written and from what is implied.
- Compare different types of narrative and information texts and identify how they are structured.
- Explore how writers use language for comic and dramatic effects.

Write for a range of purposes on paper and on screen

Strand 9 Creating and shaping texts
- Reflect independently and critically on their own writing and edit and improve it.
- Create multi-layered texts, including use of hyperlinks, linked with web pages.

Strand 10 Text structure and organisation
- Experiment with the order of sections and paragraphs to achieve different effects.
- Change the order of material within a paragraph, moving the topic sentence.

Strand 11 Sentence structure and punctuation
- Adapt sentence construction to different text-types, purposes and readers.
- Punctuate sentences accurately, including the use of speech marks and apostrophes.

Progression in persuasive writing

In this year, children are moving towards:
- Reading and evaluating letters, for example from newspapers or magazines, intended to inform, protest, complain, persuade, considering (i) how they are set out, and (ii) how language is used.
- Reading other examples (newspaper comment, headlines, adverts, fliers) to compare writing which informs and persuades, considering for example the deliberate use of ambiguity, half-truth, bias; how opinion can be disguised to seem like fact.
- Selecting and evaluating a range of texts, in print and other media, on paper

▶

UNIT 3 ◄ Persuasive texts *continued*

and on screen, for persuasiveness, clarity, quality of information.
■ Collecting and investigating the use of persuasive devices such as words and phrases; persuasive definitions; rhetorical questions; pandering, condescension, concession and deliberate ambiguities.
■ Drafting and writing individual, group or class persuasive letters for real purposes.
■ Writing a commentary on an issue on paper or screen (as a news editorial or leaflet), setting out and justifying a personal view; using structures from reading to set out and link points such as numbered lists or bullet points
■ Constructing an argument in note form or full text to persuade others of a point of view, presenting the case to the class or a group, using standard English appropriately and evaluating its effectiveness
■ Understanding how persuasive writing can be adapted for different audiences and purposes and how it can be incorporated into or combined with other text types.

Key aspects of learning covered in this Unit

Enquiry
Children will investigate how different persuasive text influence the reader.
Information processing
Children will evaluate a range of different persuasive texts that inform, protest, complain and are able to analyse their language features.
Evaluation
Children will collect and identify different persuasive devices and evaluate them for effectiveness.
Reasoning
Children will be able to give reasons for their opinions about the impact of a range of persuasive writing.
Communication
Children will draft and write different persuasive texts for real purposes in pairs or individually.

Prior learning

Before starting this Unit check that the children can:
■ Understand the purpose of persuasive writing
■ Identify a range or persuasive texts including advertisements and film trailers
■ Understand the common language features of persuasive writing.
If they need further support please refer to a prior Unit or a similar Unit in Year 4.

Resources

Come to Greece! by Mark McArthur-Christie ✇; *Stop Animal Testing!* by Chris Webster ✇; *Welcome to the Fun Zone* from www.scholastic.co.uk ✇; Persuasion skeleton ✇; *The Piano* – A film by Aidan Gibbons – web link ✇; Photographs of Parthenon, Greek Harbour and Greek Vases ✇; Photocopiable pages 157 'Persuasive phrases'; Photocopiable page 158 'Persuasive texts'; Photocopiable page 159 'Fact cards'; Photocopiable page 160 'Oral checklist cards for spoken arguments'; Assessment activity 'Car for sale!' ✇

Cross-curricular opportunities

History
ICT

UNIT 3 ■ Teaching sequence

Phase	Children's objectives	Summary of activities	Learning outcomes
1	I can analyse the use of persuasive language. I can infer writer's perspectives from what is written or implied.	Analyse the features of a persuasive text, together in class and independently. Look at a persuasive text and identify language and phrases that show the author's point of view.	Children can understand features of a persuasive text. Children can identify phrases asserting a writer's point of view.
2	I can understand how writers use persuasive language for different effects. I can present a spoken argument, sequencing points logically. I can make notes to draft a persuasive text, sequencing points logically. I can experiment with the order of sections and paragraphs to achieve different effects.	Collect phrases and different writing techniques used in three different persuasive texts. Create arguments for inclusion in a letter from the headteacher to persuade parents to send their children to the school. Feed back orally. Write first draft of a letter to parents, sequencing points logically and developing back-up points. Write the letter to persuade parents that the school is a good one. Draft two versions with paragraphs and sentences in different orders.	Children can understand how language is used for different purposes in persuasive texts. Children can develop a persuasive argument, using notes and feedback. Children can refer to own notes and draft a persuasive letter. Children can revise letter to parents with paragraphs changed and order experimented with.
3	I can make notes and use evidence from a text to persuade others. I can make notes and use evidence from a text to persuade others. I can understand different ways to take the lead and support others in groups I can understand the process of decision making. I can present a spoken argument, sequencing points, logically defending views with evidence and making use of persuasive language. I can punctuate sentences accurately, including the use of the apostrophe. I can adapt sentence construction. I can create multi-layered texts, including the use of hyperlinks. I can experiment with the order of paragraphs to achieve different effects.	Discuss the purpose of a review. Plan a review of a familiar book or film and feed back orally. Write a review of a film using personal opinion backed up with reasons that justify points of view. In groups, research and draft points for an argument about a set issue. Rehearse and present arguments for the issues. Evaluate other groups' presentations. Revise the use of the apostrophe through oral work and adapt opening paragraphs of writing for different audiences. Write own persuasive flyer about the issue researched and discussed. Evaluate the written arguments, discuss effectiveness, and revise the order of paragraphs.	Children can give an oral review of a book or film. Children can write a review of a film. Children can draft an argument, backed up with relevant information. Children can present a spoken argument on a given issue and evaluate the presentation of others. Children can write an introductory paragraph for the issue, aimed at a specific audience. Children can create a flyer of their issue using a computer program. Children can complete two versions of their flyer and evaluate them for effectiveness.

Provide copies of the objectives for the children.

DAY 1 ■ What is persuasive writing?

Key features	Stages	Additional opportunities
Enquiry: investigate persuasive texts	**Introduction** Explain to the children that this Unit is about persuasive writing. Ask them to consider the meaning of persuasion. Use paired talk to discuss times when they have persuaded someone to do something – what did they do? Take brief feedback. Look together at *Come to Greece!* from the CD-ROM and discuss the purpose of the text and its intended audience. Using shared reading, identify with the children the different language features and structure of the text. Highlight the following on the text: each paragraph identifies a different aspect of Greece; the use of exaggerated language; a summary line at the beginning of each paragraph identifying what the next argument is going to be; the use of different punctuation marks.	**Further work:** reinforce correct grammar, such as comma usage, having identified common errors from marking children's work
	Independent work Provide the children with copies of the text and ask them to identify the following by text-marking and working together: ■ the four main arguments for going to Greece ■ any additional reasons for going to Greece that are expanded on ■ six persuasive phrases that they think are really effective.	**Extend:** ensure the children find all the different aspects of the text structure
Reasoning: give reasons for their opinions	**Plenary** Bring the whole class back together and discuss whether the text persuaded them to go. If so, what was it that made them want to go? If not, why not? Discuss what type of text it is (it is from a brochure). Identify other examples of persuasive writing for example: adverts, letters of complaint, commentaries.	**Support:** provide a specific list of key aspects for the children to identify, such as connectives to join ideas, phrases that persuade you

DAY 2 ■ A writer's point of view

Key features	Stages	Additional opportunities
Enquiry: investigate persuasive texts	**Introduction** Recap with the children the purpose of persuasive writing. Explain that persuasion can change people's points of view about an important issue. Show the children *Stop Animal Testing!* from the CD-ROM. Read the text with them. Identify the main facts of the issue. Explain any unfamiliar vocabulary, such as *biological, statistic, agricultural*. Ask the children to discuss why people might think this is an important issue. Take brief feedback and record ideas on the board. Identify whether the author of the writing is *for* or *against* animal testing. Explain that this text shows only one side of the argument, and use paired talk to consider the opposing arguments in favour of animal testing. Take brief feedback on this. Show the children how the text has been structured into point, elaboration, point, elaboration.	**Further work:** discuss with children the different facts that have been collected and used in this text to enhance the argument
Reasoning: give reasons for their opinions	**Independent work** Provide the children with copies of *Stop Animal Testing!* from the CD-ROM and ask them, in pairs, to identify the different phrases that they think shows the author's viewpoint or opinion, for example *tests are cruel; tests are outdated and unnecessary*. Give them copies of the persuasion skeleton from the CD-ROM to help with their work.	**Extend:** ask children to take the text and break it down into note form
	Plenary Take feedback, recording on a chart the phrases the children think shows the author's viewpoint. Discuss the fact that you can argue a viewpoint without necessarily believing it yourself.	**Support:** provide children with a cut up version of the text and let them structure it into points and elaboration

Guided reading

Read a number of non-fiction texts that raise issues with the children. Help them to identify how the text puts across the point of view by discussing the following:

- the structure of the argument
- the amount of facts used to back the argument up and make it stronger
- the way the author shows his/her point of view, or not.

Assessment

Through oral discussion, informally assess the children's understanding of the genre by listening to their responses in whole-class and group discussion.

Refer back to the learning outcomes on page 147.

Further work

Ask the children to research a number of issues, looking for the *for* and *against* arguments. For example, fox hunting, recycling, healthy school dinners.

DAY 1 ■ Effective persuasive phrases

Key features	Stages	Additional opportunities
Enquiry: investigate how different persuasive texts influence the reader	**Introduction** Return to the text *Come to Greece!* from the CD-ROM. Discuss with the children what emotions and feelings the writer wants the reader to have in order for them to book a holiday. Identify key words: *warm, exciting, fascinating.* Discuss the different types of phrases that will create these feelings in the reader such as *Greece is amazing!*, *amid breathtaking scenery.* Discuss whether the claims are actually true – or has the writer chosen the language for a specific reason? Explain that they may be true but they have been exaggerated to get people to make the booking. Look at *Stop Animal Testing!* text from the CD-ROM. Discuss what the author has done here to make the reader respond. Press for answers that include the emotions, shock, outrage. Discuss how the author has achieved this (through extreme facts, horrific detail). Highlight a few examples.	**Support:** support the children's spelling development by using spelling journals to identify misspelled words and strategies to correct them **Extend:** ask children to select phrases that are persuasive by themselves from *Welcome to the Fun Zone!* from the CD-ROM
Evaluation: collect and identify different persuasive devices	**Independent work** Provide the children with copies of the two texts above, plus *Welcome to the Fun Zone!* from the CD-ROM. Ask them to identify all the phrases that are persuasive and then, using photocopiable page 157 'Persuasive phrases', categorise them into the emotions they raise (shock, outrage, anger and so on). **Plenary** Draw a three-column grid on the board with the headings of the emotions that the children were asked to identify. Discuss why the writers have used the tactic of raising each particular emotion.	**Support:** provide key words and phrases that you want the children to scan for and explain

DAY 2 ■ Planning a persuasive text

Key features	Stages	Additional opportunities
Reasoning: give reasons for their opinions	**Introduction** Explain to the children that they are going to begin to put together their own persuasive text. Tell them that the headteacher needs to put together a new letter to persuade parents to send their children to the school. Using an enlarged version of the Persuasion skeleton from the CD-ROM, discuss briefly the different aspects of the school. Ask the children, in pairs, to consider what things a parent would be looking for, take feedback and record the ideas on the board. Keep this list for 'Independent work'. In pairs, ask the children to discuss ideas for four main points for their letter to parents. Take feedback and make notes on one of the issues, focusing the children's attention on the back-up arguments that will be needed in the paragraph. (Keep a copy.)	**Support:** provide the children with examples of persuasive language and different connectives to link their ideas together: *another reason; children at this school are; the school is known as.* **Extend:** ask the children to develop their ideas in note form ready to use to express arguments orally
Communication: draft persuasive text for real purposes	**Independent work** Print copies of the Persuasion skeleton from the CD-ROM for the children and give them access to the list of parental requirements created in the whole-class work. In pairs, ask them to make notes on their main points to persuade parents to send their children to the school, such as excellent facilities, after school clubs. Ask them to rehearse their points so they can provide oral feedback. Remind them to organise their arguments in a logical manner. **Plenary** Select groups to feed back on their points. Encourage them to give a summary of each main point before providing back-up arguments.	**Support:** let children plan their reasons in a guided session

DAY 3 ▪ Drafting own letter to parents

Key features	Stages	Additional opportunities
	### Introduction	
Reasoning: give reasons for their opinions	Using the main points outlined from Day 2, model for the children how to structure the notes made in class into a coherent persuasive text. Remind them of the different persuasive phrases that they identified on Day 1. What emotions and thoughts do they want the readers of the letter to parents to have? Then discuss which subject it would be the best to start with. If necessary back up each point you write with facts such as the number of teachers, specialists, results, trips and so on. Model the first two paragraphs, following a similar structure to that of *Come to Greece!* from the CD-ROM.	**Support:** revise different appropriate connectives to use in this text, such as *In addition..., Have you heard how amazing..., As well as this...*
Evaluation: identify different persuasive devices	Show the children how to create summary lines, for example: *The children at Clewer Green School are well taught* or *Every term the school organises fun and exciting events.* As you write, discuss with the children how points made in a paragraph all link to the summary statement at the start. Model key writing techniques such as re-reading the writing to check for punctuation; changing and rephrasing sentences before writing and so on.	**Extend:** focus children on developing their elaborations so their points are expanded
Communication: draft and write persuasive texts for real purposes	### Independent work Provide the children with their notes from Day 2 and allow time for them to discuss the order of their arguments. Do these link to the most important things the readers will be looking for? Ask the children to then draft their version of the letter to parents. (Keep copies of their work.)	**Support:** provide a frame for the children's writing with starters, such as: *Another reason..., This means that...*
	### Plenary Invite children to read out their most effective phrase. Would you send your child to the school?	

DAY 4 ▪ Developing ideas within a paragraph

Key features	Stages	Additional opportunities
	### Introduction	
Reasoning: give reasons for their opinions	Return to the text *Come to Greece!* from the CD-ROM. Discuss with the children how persuasive it would sound if the paragraphs were in a different order. Read the text in a different order. Discuss the changes. Are you, as the reader, more interested or less? Use an example of the children's writing of the letter to parents from Day 3. Identify through shared reading the different arguments that the children have used to persuade readers to send their children to the school. Have they put the strongest reason first and have they backed it up? Ask them to discuss whether the writing in the paragraph shows the argument in the strongest way. Draw the children's attention to the order of the ideas and reasons, the connecting phrases that have been used and the exaggerated language. Take their suggestions and redraft the paragraph. Identify the reasons why the newer version is stronger than the previous version, for example, the sentences are ordered more logically and are more clearly expressed. Discuss different ways to rephrase sentences.	**Support:** remind and reinforce the use of commas within a sentence to add clarity to writing **Extend:** ask children to revise all their paragraphs to complete the letter
Communication: draft and write persuasive texts for real purposes	### Independent work Ask the children to return to their first main point in their letter to parents and redraft it, putting the strongest argument first and then clarifying the sequence of sentences so the ideas progress logically and makes sense.	**Support:** provide the children with sentences from a paragraph chopped up so they can explore the effects of the organisation of sentences
	### Plenary Invite the children to re-read their first version and then their new version of the paragraph and identify what they have done to improve it.	

Guided reading

When reading non-fiction texts with the children, identify with them how ideas are developed in paragraphs by:
■ the use of a general sentence that summarises what the paragraph is about
■ the subsequent sentences following a clear logical pattern that takes the reader through the main ideas of the writer.
Encourage the children to identify this technique in different genres, for example, report texts and so on.

Assessment

Using observation, discussion and teacher marking, informally assess the children's understanding of and application in writing the features of the genre.
Identify further teaching points for the next Phase.
Refer back to the learning outcomes on page 147.

Further work

Ask the children to collect different examples of persuasive texts from flyers to websites to junk mail, from television advertisements to brochures and so on. Ask them to identify the purpose, audience and language features of each. How do they differ for different audiences?

DAY 1 ◼ Writing film reviews

Key features	Stages	Additional opportunities
Enquiry: investigate how persuasive texts influence the reader	**Introduction** Explain the concept of reviewing to the children, that is: someone sees a film or reads a book and then recommends to others whether they should see it or read it. Use paired talk to encourage the children to identify an example of a book or a film that they have seen and explain why they would recommend it. Take brief feedback and, from the discussions, identify that when recommending books or films you describe the story or plot of it and which bits are good and why. Identify from the children's oral contributions that they have also given examples of incidents or special effects that were particularly good. Show them an example of a review from a web page. Discuss how the review is structured. Identify with them any similarities between this and the persuasive structure. In what way is this review persuasive writing? Take brief feedback.	**Extend:** discuss strategies to remember the spellings of tricky words through identification of patterns, mnemonics and syllables **Extend:** focus on the development of the reviewer's opinion, designed to capture attention
	Independent work Adapt photocopiable page 158 'Persuasive texts' for the children to put together their reasons for recommending a book or film of their own choice. Encourage them to structure their recommendations to include a summary of the plot. Tell them they need to be able to give their review orally at the end of the lesson.	
Reasoning: give reasons for their opinions	**Plenary** Choose a number of children put their reviews forward to the class. Discuss with the audience whether the reviewer has persuaded them to go and see the film or read the book.	**Support:** focus on the use of connectives, such as *therefore* and *another reason*

DAY 2 ◼ Writing a film review

Key features	Stages	Additional opportunities
Enquiry: investigate persuasive texts **Reasoning:** give reasons for their opinions	**Introduction** Use the film *The Piano* by Aidan Gibbons (there is a web link to this resource on the CD-ROM). The children will be familiar with this film if they have covered Fiction Unit 5, 'Film narrative'. Play the film to the children, asking them to notice key facts about the film, from both the film itself and the opening titles and credits, such as who made it, where it was made and the date. Using photocopiable page 158 'Persuasive texts' as a structure, outline with the children an example of notes that they would use to create a positive review (they liked it). Identify what key facts about the film they would want to use: for example: title, maker, where it was filmed, style, subject matter. Discuss with the children what changes they would need to make to the structure of the positive argument to make it a negative viewpoint. Remind them of some of the different headings they noticed when looking at the review website yesterday. Show the children how to use the same headings to show viewpoints that are both for and against the film.	**Support:** remind the children to include key facts about the film from their knowledge and the film itself **Extend:** focus on developing a reviewing style, such as *If you like wartime movies then you are in for a treat!*
Evaluation: evaluate persuasive devices	**Independent work** Ask the children to use their own notes to write a review of the film, choosing the viewpoint to write from. **Plenary** Share the reviews together. How effectively have the children conveyed their viewpoints?	**Support:** provide the children with a frame to support their writing with headings

DAY 3 ◢ My opinion is best!

Key features	Stages	Additional opportunities
Reasoning: give reasons for their opinions **Information processing:** evaluate persuasive texts	### Introduction Explain to the children that over the next five lessons they are going to prepare, in groups, an argument presenting a point of view for an issue that will eventually become a written piece of text like the *Stop Animal Testing!* flyer (from the CD-ROM). Say that they will work in groups of three or four to come up with well researched arguments to present to the class. Provide them with copies of photocopiable page 158 'Persuasive texts', a relevant card from a cut up version of photocopiable page 159 'Fact cards' and paper for notes. Remind the children that they are going to need to work collaboratively to get the best ideas for their arguments. Show them an enlarged version of photocopiable page 159 and explain the issues. Briefly discuss with them what the key arguments *for* and *against* the issues would be and record these on a flipchart. Say that in order to make their arguments stronger, the children will need to back up their ideas with facts. Explain that some of the facts have website links to help research. Outline the time frame for the task. ### Independent work Split the children into groups of three or four and allow them access to the internet, if necessary, to plan their arguments. Remind them to agree on whether they are arguing for or against the point of view. (Keep copies of the children's notes on photocopiable page 158 for future use.) ### Plenary Discuss with the children how they reached agreement on their arguments.	**Support:** remind the children of the key rules for working collaboratively: listening, negotiating, presenting an alternative viewpoint calmly, offering suggestions, taking and identifying roles in the groups **Extend:** remind the children about note-taking strategies to ensure accurate facts and references **Support:** provide a note-taking sheet to support the children in finding facts to back up their arguments

DAY 4 ◢ Presenting a spoken argument

Key features	Stages	Additional opportunities
Reasoning: give reasons for their opinions **Evaluation:** identify persuasive devices and evaluate them for effectiveness	### Introduction Refer back to *Stop Animal Testing!* (from the CD-ROM). Remind the children that they need to be really clear about their arguments. Re-read the text together, pointing out aspects of the structure that help create a coherent argument or point of view (a separate paragraph outlining the facts about the issue; simple connectives indicating the order of the key points such as *first* and *secondly*; examples provided including facts to back up the argument). Explain to the children that they will need to work on putting their arguments together so that they run logically. Tell them they should decide who is going to outline the issue, present argument 1, argument 2 and so on. Remind them that it is really important to back up their points as far as they can with facts. ### Speaking and listening Provide the children with a short time frame in which they are to rehearse their points of view about the issue. When rehearsing, tell them to evaluate each part of their argument to see if it has the following: ■ a clear introduction outlining the issue ■ each point in order, with information and facts to back it up and expand upon it. At the end of the time limit, ask each group to present their viewpoint to the rest of the class. ### Plenary Allow the children time to evaluate the presentations, using photocopiable page 160 'Oral checklist cards for spoken arguments'.	**Extend:** provide children with time to evaluate their own group performance in working together collaboratively **Extend:** draft a frame for children to use to record their arguments **Support:** provide teaching assistant support to the group to ensure that their arguments are clear

DAY 5 ■ Apostrophes, commas and other punctuation

Key features	Stages	Additional opportunities
Reasoning: give reasons for their opinions	### Introduction Prepare in advance some 'Show me' cards (for children to show in response to a question) that have *P* (possessive) or *O* (omission) marked on them. Say part of a sentence that contains an apostrophe and ask the children to show you which type of apostrophe it is, for example *The cat's food was all eaten* (possessive *P*). Ask them to explain their reasoning. Repeat with a number of other sentences. Reverse the procedure asking the children to write the sentence down showing the correct written model, for example (oral sentence from the teacher), *Sarah couldn't find her coat at the end of the day*. Repeat for a number of sentences. Provide the children with different audiences, for example younger sister, parent, older sibling. Discuss how they would write a paragraph outlining the issue they are investigating so that this person would understand it. Discuss the types of sentences, vocabulary and facts to include.	**Extend:** revise the use of commas within complex sentences then ask the children to write a paragraph to suit two different audiences
Communication: write persuasive texts for real purposes	### Independent work Ask the children to write their own introduction to their issue for a specific audience. ### Plenary Take feedback from the children on the sentences they used and discuss the differences.	**Support:** use a guided writing session to focus the children on writing their paragraph

DAY 6 ■ Creating a flyer using ICT

Key features	Stages	Additional opportunities
	### Introduction This lesson can be done in an ICT suite or with access to computers. Provide the children with copies of the notes they made on photocopiable page 158 'Persuasive texts' for their spoken arguments relating to their issue (Days 3 and 4). Explain to them that they are going to draft their completed written version of their viewpoint directly onto a word-processing, publishing or multimedia program so that it looks like a flyer similar to *Stop Animal Testing* from the CD-ROM. Remind them of the important aspects of persuasive writing you are looking for: ■ a clear introduction outlining the issue ■ strong points in logical order ■ each point developed and backed up with facts and examples ■ connectives used to link ideas together with children not using them more than once ■ paragraphs clearly outlined ■ fonts to engage the reader and capture the attention	**ICT:** make simple observations of how well children can apply ICT skills in another curriculum area **Extend:** encourage children to use all the facilities on the computer to enhance their flyers
Communication: write persuasive texts for real purposes	### Independent work Ask the children to create their own flyer collaboratively. Remind them that they can insert images to make their flyer more powerful in its message. ### Plenary At the end of the lesson allow the children to look at one another's work. Briefly discuss which one grabs the attention.	**Support:** provide a structured frame on the computer into which children can insert their arguments and modify fonts

DAY 7 ◼ Changing the order of my argument

Key features	Stages	Additional opportunities
Communication: write different persuasive texts	**Introduction** Print out a number of examples of the children's written flyers. Provide them with copies. Ask them to evaluate the quality of the persuasive flyer by considering how effectively: ■ the argument is put across ■ the main points express the point of view ■ the images or fonts capture the attention of the reader ■ the argument develops and expands as it is read ■ the facts strengthen the argument. Ask the children to provide feedback on these and to make constructive suggestions for improvements. Discuss how reordering the sections and paragraphs might give a different viewpoint. Using a word-processing package, model for the children how to make changes to the order of the paragraphs by moving text around and then saving it as a different version.	**Extend:** children provide detailed reasons for why they made the changes and why one text is more effective than the other
Evaluation: identify different persuasive devices and evaluate them for effectiveness	**Independent work** Using a word-processing package, ask the children to create a second version of their flyer by reorganising the order of the paragraphs. Encourage the children to consider whether the changes they have made have strengthened the flyer's argument or weakened it. **Plenary** Print off the two versions of the text and ask the children to compare them.	**Support:** children provide oral reasons for the changes they made

Guided reading
Read a range of non-fiction texts, focusing the children's attention on the following :
■ the order of sections and paragraphs in the text
■ how illustrations and photographs aid the reader
■ how the writer organises the facts to make the writing coherent.

Assessment
Use the assessment task 'Car for sale' from the CD-ROM to formally assess the children's understanding of the genre of persuasion.
Refer back to the learning outcomes on page 147.

Further work
Run mini class debating sessions at story time, allowing the children to practise putting forward their points of view logically, using key connectives to link ideas together such as:
■ *some people think*
■ *nevertheless*
■ *in addition to.*

Persuasive phrases

■ Read the persuasive texts that you have been given. Identify the persuasive phrases and categorise them according to the emotion that they raise by writing them in the appropriate box.

Different emotions	Phrases that evoke the emotion
Anger, shock, outrage	
Longing, wishing	
Amazing, fantastic	

NON-FICTION ■ UNIT 3

Persuasive texts

This is an outline of the issue

Some of the key facts

I agree/disagree with this issue because

Main reason

Elaboration

A second reason

Elaboration

A third reason

Elaboration

PHOTOCOPIABLE

Fact cards

Issue 1. Should chips be banned from school?

FACTS

1. 1 in 23 children are classified as obese.
2. Obesity in children affects children's health later in life.
3. Obesity is linked to heart disease.
4. Portion sizes have got bigger and fast food is everywhere.
5. It is recommended we eat five portions of fruit and veg a day.

Issue 2. Should mobile phones be banned from children under 12?

FACTS

1. 70% children between the ages of 10-14 own a mobile phone.
2. Doctors fear that children suffer brain damage from phones, though this isn't proven.
3. School staff think that children are more vulnerable to bullying and theft if they have a phone.

Issue 3. Should children as young as 6 be given homework?

FACTS

1. The government says that homework is important as it raises the level of achievement of children.
2. Recommended homework for KS1 is the subjects of reading, literacy and numeracy.
3. Homework should be set two times a week.
4. Activities should be linked to work in class and should be things children can do.

Issue 4. Should every school recycle its rubbish?

FACTS

1. 28 million tonnes of rubbish leave our homes each year.
2. In a week we produce enough rubbish to fill Wembey Stadium. Over half of this rubbish can be recycled.
3. Every tonne of paper recycled saves 17 trees.
4. The world's energy resources are dwindling.

Name _____ Date _____

Oral checklist cards for spoken arguments

■ Listen to the other group's arguments/presentation of their issues. After you have listened carefully to their point of view consider the following questions to support the feedback you give them.

■ Did they outline the issue clearly so the audience understood?

YES/NO

■ Did the group clearly show whether they were *for* or *against* the issue?

YES/NO

■ Did the group put forward three clear reasons for their point of view?

YES/NO

■ Did the group back up each reason they stated with evidence, for example facts or more reasons that explained what they thought?

YES/NO

Prepare general feedback to the group that presented

Two positive things about how the group presented the argument.

■ _____

_____

■ _____

_____

One thing that they could work on.

■ _____

_____

POETRY
UNIT 1 Poetic style

Read for a range of purposes on paper and on screen

Strand 7 Understanding and interpreting texts
- Make notes on and use evidence from across a text to explain events or ideas.
- Infer writers' perspectives from what is written and from what is implied.
- Explore how writers use language for comic and dramatic effects.

Strand 8 Engaging with and responding to texts
- Reflect on reading habits and preferences and plan personal reading goals.
- Compare the usefulness of techniques, such as visualisation, prediction, empathy in exploring the meaning of texts.
- Compare how a common theme is presented in poetry, prose and other media.

Write for a range of purposes on paper and on screen

Strand 9 Creating and shaping texts
- Reflect independently and critically on own writing and edit and improve it.
- Adapt non-narrative forms and styles to write fiction or factual texts, including poems.

Strand 12 Presentation
- Adapt handwriting for specific purposes, for example printing, use of italics.
- Use a range of ICT programs to present texts, making informed choices of which electronic tools to use for different purposes.

Progression in poetry

In this year, children are moving towards:
- Discussing a poet's possible viewpoint, explaining and justifying their own responses and interpretation.
- Explaining the use of unusual or surprising language choices and effects, such as onomatopoeia and metaphor; commenting on how this influences meaning.
- Exploring imagery including metaphor and personification.
- Comparing different forms and describing the impact.
- Inventing nonsense words and situations and experimenting with unexpected word combinations.
- Using carefully observed details and apt images to bring subject matter alive.
- Writing free verse, poems using or inventing repeating patterns and attempting different forms.

▶

Key aspects of learning covered in this Unit

Enquiry
Children will investigate an older narrative poem, seeking the answers to their own and others' questions. They will engage in drama and discussion and then plan and present their own version orally and visually.

Information processing
Children will identify relevant information from a range of sources and use this as a basis for a choral performance of their own version of the poem.

Evaluation
Children will present information orally, through drama and in writing. They will discuss success criteria, give feedback to others and judge the effectiveness of their own work.

Self-awareness
Children will discuss and reflect on their personal responses to the poems.

Communication
Children will develop their skills to reflect critically on what they have seen and read. They will develop their ability to present a poem orally and reflect critically on their own and others' work.

Prior learning

Before starting this Unit check that the children can:
■ Identify similes and other simple images; explain their use in creating vivid word pictures.
■ Understand the characteristics of poetry and know different forms and structures.
■ Know vocabulary related to poetic form such as verse, rhyme, couplet and so on.
■ Have knowledge of different types of poem: Free verse, haiku, cinquain, acrostic and so on.
If they need further support please refer to a prior Unit or a similar Unit in Year 4.

Resources

The Frozen Man by Kit Wright ✎; *All of Us* by Kit Wright ✎; *Cold Morning* by Celia Warren ✎; *I saw a peacock* by Anon ✎; Photocopiable page 171 'The Frozen Man'; Photocopiable page 172 'Poetic style'; Photographs of the Sun and Moon ✎; Assessment activity 'My progress with poetry' ✎

Cross-curricular opportunities

Geography

UNIT 1 ■ Teaching sequence

Phase	Children's objectives	Summary of activities	Learning outcomes
1	I can explain why an author chose particular words to express an idea. I can identify and create metaphors and similes. I can identify how particular words are chosen for their precise meaning.	Use *The Frozen Man*. Whole-class reading and analysing of text for word effects. Discuss and record ideas. Children use photocopiable page to record and explain their understanding of the imagery. Use *The Frozen Man* to identify metaphors. Children discuss metaphors using pictures from CD-ROM. They write their own similes and metaphors independently. Use *Cold Morning* to see if children can identify metaphors. Texts: *The Frozen Man, Cold Morning, I saw a peacock*. Discussion of the texts and how words are chosen and used in the writing. The children select sentences and phrases, explaining why they like them.	Children can record and explain their understanding of the imagery in a poem. Children can create metaphors from pictures and images on the board. Children can identify and explain their preferences for certain phrases.
2	I can respond to poems explaining preferences. I can compare the structure and language of two poems by different writers. I can identify different structures used by writers to write poetry.	Texts: *Cold Morning; The Frozen Man; I saw a peacock*. Identify with the children what the writers are trying to say. The children write, expressing their own preferences for poems, and brainstorm ideas for writing their own poetry. Texts: *Cold Morning; The Frozen Man*. Compare the two poems according to specific criteria, ie structure, content and word choices. *The Frozen Man /All of Us/ I saw a peacock*. Analysis of the text structure of these three poems so children can use them in their own writing. In pairs, the children use some of the structures to begin to experiment with ideas.	Children can write a journal entry expressing preferences. Children can identify similarities and differences in form and language features used. Children can understand the different structures used for different poems.
3	I can analyse and write own poems using structures and techniques identified. I can refine and redraft poems, focusing on word choice. I can write my own poem selecting structure and content. I can refine work for publication.	Use shared writing to model the start of the poem based on the structure of *The Frozen Man* – ie two distinct and contrasting sections. The teacher models for the children how to refine their poems, focusing on the word choice. Children in response identify words that they can improve upon. The teacher supports the children to select their own poem and structure to write about, based on their own experience. Using shared writing, teacher models a poem applying the techniques of word choices in the writing. The teacher models for the children how to edit their writing by selecting key words and phrases to refine and improve. The children create a final version of their poem ready for publication. They then share their redrafted poems with the class.	Children can produce a first draft of collaborative poems based on *The Frozen Man* or another poem read. Children can revise first drafts of poems and improve them by focusing on word choice. Children can write own poem based on own experiences or a person using a structure of choice. Children can refine own verse and make a final copy for publication.

Provide copies of the objectives for the children.

DAY 1 ▪ The Frozen Man

Key features	Stages	Additional opportunities
Self-awareness: discuss and reflect on personal responses to poems	**Introduction** Use paired talk to explore what the children already know about poetry. Record their ideas on a board. Key questions are: How is it different to story writing? What poetic structures do they know? What techniques do writers use when they write poetry? Focus on vocabulary such as rhyme, alliteration, pattern, and simile. Identify with the children that poets write about all kinds of different things, some from their own experience. Outline that the Unit is going to look at the work of two key writers. Introduce the first poem: *The Frozen Man* from the CD-ROM. Use paired talk to discuss what this frozen man might look like. Read the poem aloud to the children. Key questions for discussion are: *What is the poem about? What is the poet trying to say?* Identify with the children words and phrases such as: *black trees crack their fingers, breath of cattle still as boulders*. Discuss why the author chose 'crack their fingers' and 'still as boulders'. Identify that the poem is structured in two parts and that these parts contrast. **Independent work** Children use photocopiable page 171 'The Frozen Man' to identify words and phrases in the text that powerfully convey the contrast between the outside and the inside parts of the poem. Encourage the children to write down what pictures come into their heads from reading them. **Plenary** Introduce to children that the author uses a technique called metaphor to bring to life an object that he is describing. Explain that a metaphor is a device to compare something to something else that is similar to it, for example *where black trees crack their fingers in the icy wind*. What are the trees' fingers? Can the children find any other examples?	**Spelling:** revise the rules for doubling letters when *-ed* and *-ing* are added. Alternatively, focus time on revising the *-ou-/-ough/-ow* phoneme in longer words requiring syllabification strategies **Extend:** provide opportunities to make deeper inferences from the poems **Support:** allow the children to express preferences and explain specific vocabulary

DAY 2 ▪ What is a metaphor?

Key features	Stages	Additional opportunities
Enquiry: understanding how similes and metaphors are created	**Introduction** Return to *The Frozen Man* and recap the children's ideas. Invite them to scan yesterday's text to find some more metaphors. Explain that *you can hear the warmth like a sleeping cat* is a simile, because the comparison starts with *like*. Discuss some other similes. Show the children the range of pictures from the CD-ROM and think of objects and items that they could be compared to. Discuss with the children which kinds of comparisons are likely and effective because they make logical sense. For example, *My fingers run like a cheetah* may not be as appropriate as *He ran as swiftly as a cheetah*. **Independent work** Show the children other pictures and ask them to create a range of appropriate similes. **Plenary** Introduce the poem *Cold Morning*. Read it aloud and invite the children to spot the metaphor in it (Joyous flag). Identify the differences between a simile and a metaphor.	**Extend:** provide the children with an additional text, such as *All of Us* by Kit Wright, and ask them to identify and explain the metaphors **Support:** just create similes by making simple comparisons with like/as

DAY 3 ■ Choosing the best word

Key features	Stages	Additional opportunities
Enquiry: identifying how authors use of language creates effects	## Introduction Return to the text *The Frozen Man*. Remind the children that, as the readers, they are able to express preferences for whether they like it or not. Remind them that authors choose words specifically because they are trying to communicate to the reader a specific picture. Ask the children, in pairs, to pick two of the phrases from the poem that they particularly like and ask them to explain why. Record these on the text. Show the children *I saw a peacock* from the CD-ROM and read it aloud to them. Ask them to discuss the poem's patterns and language, and then focus their talk on their preferences regarding the language used. Do the same for the poem *Cold Morning*, recording on the text the children's favourite lines and phrases.	work on synonyms, using a thesaurus to find words with shades of meaning
Information processing: discussing poems read	## Independent work Provide the children with copies of the poems *Cold Morning*, *The Frozen Man* and *I saw a peacock*. Ask them to underline phrases that they like and, in their books, ask them to explain why they are good phrases to use and why they like them. Remind the children that they need to explain in words the pictures they get in their heads.	**Extend:** identify the use of similes and metaphors in two different poems and explain their effects
	## Plenary Provide the children with a simple sentence on the board. Invite them to improve the sentence by adding some of the following: precise nouns, similes, powerful verbs, metaphors and adjectives. Discuss the improvements and how different words create different meanings.	**Support:** provide a section of the poem to read and key phrases to scan for, underline and explain

Guided reading

Use the Unit to support the teaching of word choices and language effects that will link to assessment focus 5 in the National Tests at KS2.
Targets for reading could be:
■ To identify the use of descriptive language in poetry and describe the effect it has.
■ To understand the difference between literal and figurative language in poetry and prose.

Assessment

Informally assess the children's ability to explain imagery and word effect orally.
Assess their ability to explain images through marking their books, and carry out closer assessment of key groups through guided reading. Add in questions that focus on an author's word choices and assess the children's responses.
Refer back to the learning outcomes on page 163.

Further work

Read a selection of poems by Kit Wright and Celia Warren to the children at other times during the day.
Children can access information about the writers on the Internet.
For homework, ask the children to select their own favourite poems for a class anthology.

DAY 1 ■ What do writers write poems about?

Key features	Stages	Additional opportunities
Enquiry: contrast and respond to poems from two significant writers	**Introduction** Provide the children with copies of the three poems looked at yesterday. Identify with them what the writer is trying to say in each and discuss why the poems might have been written. Record the ideas on a chart on a board. For example, *Cold Morning* is about a dog that perhaps the writer had and is missing. *The Frozen Man* might be about someone the writer had seen on a very cold night or might have come from his own experiences. Ask the children to say why they like a particular poem, for example they might like *I saw a peacock* because it repeats and has rhymes. For each response ask them to explain, referring to the structure and language of the text. Tell them it is OK not to like it as long as they can justify their reasons. Discuss different ideas that the children could have for writing their own poems and record these on the board. Use paired talk to suggest key questions. For example, can they think of when they have felt outside of something and then drawn in (link with *The Frozen Man*) or when they felt cold, then warm? Can they think of something they miss or have lost that they would like to have back? Can they think of lots of things that they would just like to make rhymes up about? Tell them that they are going to need to refer back to these later on in the Unit. **Independent work** The children write their preferences in their books for each of the poems, giving reasons, along with a list of suggested items that they could use in their writing. **Plenary** Take brief feedback from the children on their ideas and explain they are going to use these later in the Unit.	identify opportunities for developing the children's vocabulary thought the use of new words, such as joyous, brimful, gnawing greatcoat discuss strategies for spelling some of these words **Extend:** let the children write a comparison between the works of the two authors **Support:** provide a structured frame to support the children's thinking

DAY 2 ■ What do writers do that is the same?

Key features	Stages	Additional opportunities
Enquiry: contrast and respond to poems from two significant writers	**Introduction** Refer to the three poems *The Frozen Man, Cold Morning* and *I saw a peacock* again. Draw a chart on the board that has similar layout to photocopiable page 172 'Poetic style'. Begin to make comparisons with the children of two of the poems in terms of layout and organisation, language effects (such as powerful verbs, metaphors), content, structure and so on. Model for the children how to make the comparisons. Explain that writers sometimes use the same techniques to achieve similar effects and that they are looking for these in the poems. **Independent work** Provide the children with copies of photocopiable page 172 'Poetic style', and ask them to refer to copies of the texts to make comparisons. **Plenary** Get feedback from the children about similarities and differences of the structure and style of the poems. Can they find examples of the same technique? Is the effect the same in each poem? Why not? (This is usually because it is linked to what the writer is trying to say, for example in *I saw a peacock* similes are used for fun). Focus on the structure and organisation. Which structure is easier to use? Draw together a list of different techniques used, such as metaphors, similes, alliteration, repetition and so on.	provide children with other poems that are known to them, perhaps from an anthology, and see if the can identify the structure **Extend:** compare a known and an unknown poem **Support:** provide the children with a copy of a familiar poem and a grid to identify the language features

DAY 3 ■ What's the structure?

Key features	Stages	Additional opportunities
Enquiry: identify different structures used by writers to write poetry	### Introduction Show the children a number of different openings to poems that reflect the structure of those studied, particularly focusing on *The Frozen Man* and *I saw a peacock.* Suggested poems to write could be: *I am the tree standing as tall as a tower*　　*At the edge of the field* *I am the tower that has stood on the hill*　　*Where the cold children* *I saw a willow bending in the wind*　　　　　*Stand with frozen knees* 　　　　　　　　　　　　　　　　　　　　　*Prickling in the air* Ask children to identify what the different structures are. Using individual whiteboards and working in pairs, invite them to create their own start to a poem that uses the same structure as each of the poems. ### Independent activity Ask the children to continue to work collaboratively together to write two short poems that have different structures, for example two verses with one contrasting to the other, or one with a repeated starting line. ### Plenary Take brief feedback from the children's writing. Show them the poem *All of Us* by Kit Wright. Ask them to read it to themselves initially, and then to think about what patterns and structure it has. Discuss with the children what they think the writer is trying to say and how the organisation of the text helps him to do it.	**Extend:** children invent their own versions of poems based on the structures identified **Support:** provide a simple frame that mirrors the structure of one of the poems for children to record

Guided reading
Use this Phase to develop children's own reading attitudes and preferences. Possible targets for groups could be:
■ To develop an active response to their own reading, for example by making comments, expressing preferences and justifying them.
■ To take part in peer group discussions and recommendations to widen their reading experience.

Assessment
Through close marking of the children's work, assess their ability to make comparisons between poems in key areas such as structure, language effects and content.
Through oral and paired work, informally assess the children's understanding of the structure of poetry.
Refer back to the learning outcomes on page 163.

Further work
Read a selection of poems by Kit Wright and Celia Warren to children at other times during the day.
Children can access information about the writers on the Internet.
For homework, ask the children to select their own favourite poems for a class anthology.

DAY 1 ▪ Writing my own version

Key features	Stages	Additional opportunities
Evaluation: analyse and write own poems using structures and techniques identified	**Introduction** Remind the children that they are familiar with the structure of the poem *The Frozen Man*. Ask them briefly to explain the structure to one another. Explain that today they are going to use the same structure to write their own poem that has two contrasting parts. Remind them to refer to their list of experiences that they could write about (Phase 2, Day 1 'What do writers write poems about?'). Using shared writing, model your own poem for the children that mirrors *The Frozen Man* because it uses the same structure. As you write, ask them to point out some of the techniques you have used and explain their effect. Remind the children that, since they are writing from their own experiences, they can draw on their memories of how they felt to convey the message to the reader.	**Extend:** the children select the structure they want to use
	Independent work The children write their own poems that follow the same structure as *The Frozen Man* or *I saw a peacock*.	**Support:** provide a guided writing session to support the children as they write their poems
	Plenary Gather the children to share in pairs what they have written. Ask them to identify the structures they have used to write their poems, ask: *Are the lines organised in pairs? Is there a contrast in the second half of the poem? Have you used a metaphor? Have you repeated any lines at the end?*	

DAY 2 ▪ Can I make my writing better?

Key features	Stages	Additional opportunities
Evaluation: to refine and redraft poems, focusing on word choice	**Introduction** Show the children models and examples of their work from yesterday. Ask the class to identify things that the writer has done successfully: Has he/she shown a contrast within the poem? Can they recognise the structure of *The Frozen Man* in the poem written? Which words has the writer used that they consider to be effective? Which ones do they consider to be weaker? In pairs, ask the children to read their work again with a response partner to identify areas where they were strong and words or phrases that they think need changing.	
	Independent work The children return to their own work to revise and edit their own writing. Provide a clear list of criteria for them to check with their reading response partner. For example, are the metaphors the best that they could be? Are the verses organised well enough? Are there capital letters at the beginning of each line? Remind them what they are trying to focus on – selecting the best word or phrase that will convey what they are trying to say. The children then create a second draft of their work.	**Extend:** provide a guided writing session that supports the redrafting process
	Plenary Discuss the changes the children have made and read out the new versions. Ask them to explain why they made the changes they did and what effect they had.	**Support:** encourage independent checking of spelling and verse structure

DAY 3 ▦ Be a poet...

Key features	Stages	Additional opportunities
Evaluation: analyse and write own poems using structures and techniques identified	### Introduction Remind the children of the different structures of the poems that they identified during Phase 2, Day 3. Explain that they are going to use these today to write their own poems. This time they are able to choose not only the content but the form that they use. Model for children two different poems that imitate the structures that the children have become familiar with - that of *Cold Morning* and *I saw a peacock*. The starting lines could be: *I saw a chameleon with its array of colours*, or *I looked out one harsh winter morning*. Model these examples reminding the children that the content comes from their own memories and experiences as well as things they have read. Ask them to explain which structures you have modelled. Remind them to refer back to their list of ideas they made for writing poems earlier in the Unit. ### Independent work The children write their own poems, choosing both the subject matter and the structure they would like to use. Remind them of different language techniques to include, for example similes, metaphors, alliteration and so on. For less confident learners, provide them with a frame or model to follow or write with them in a guided session. Encourage some children to draft straight onto the computer. ### Plenary Read the poems and invite the children to express their preferences regarding one another's writing.	**ICT:** provide some children with the opportunity to redraft using the computer, allowing them to experiment with fonts and layout to create the desired effects **Extend:** allow the children free choice about the structure of their poem but remind them to write it about something they know **Support:** children use the structure of *I saw a peacock* to write their own poems

DAY 4 ▦ ...and get published!

Key features	Stages	Additional opportunities
Evaluation: to analyse the key themes, structure, features, language of poems	### Introduction Show the class examples of different children's work. Invite them to spot tricks and techniques that have been used to good effect in the writing. Refer back to the examples of the poems you modelled for the children yesterday and discuss what changes and improvements you need to make to bring them up to publication level. Show: ■ how to change specific words ■ how to rephrase things by changing word order ■ how to move chunks of text around so that ideas are in a different order Remind the children that it is important to read what they have written aloud so that they can hear what it sounds like. ### Independent work The children work with their response partners or individually to improve and finalise their work. They then create a best copy for publication, either in writing or on the computer. ### Plenary Invite the children to perform their poems out loud. Provide them all with a few minutes' practice time before they read. Some may want to do this in pairs. The children then read their poems and the audience responds to them.	**Extend:** give children specific criteria and key areas to reflect on from your marking **Support:** allow some children to edit and redraft using a computer, experimenting with fonts and layouts

Guided writing

Use guided writing with appropriate groups to assist with the independent writing process. Provide structured frames for writing their own version of *The Frozen Man*.

Provide less confident children with a structured frame for writing poetry to support their understanding.

All the children should choose the content of their poem.

Assessment

Assess how far the children have progressed by focusing on:
- word choice and effect of words
- the structure they have chosen to use and the consistency with which they have applied it.

Assess the children's ability to write expressive and figurative language.

Give the children the assessment sheet 'My progress with poetry' from the CD-ROM to complete.

Refer back to the learning outcomes on page 163.

Further work

Read a selection of poems by Kit Wright and Celia Warren to children at other times during the day.

Children can access information about the writers on the Internet. For homework, ask the children to select their own favourite poems for a class anthology.

Name _____   Date _____

The Frozen Man

■ Read *The Frozen Man* and fill in the chart below.

Text from the poem *The Frozen Man*	Technique used by the poet Alliteration, metaphor, powerful verbs, adjective, similes	Picture I have in my head
Black trees crack their fingers		
Icy wind		
Hedges freeze on their shadows		
Under the rolling moon		
On the coal-black road		
You can hear the warmth like a sleeping cat		
Let him in, Let him in, Let him in		

Name _____   Date _____

Poetic style

■ Compare the three poems and write about them in the columns below.

	The Frozen Man	Cold Morning	I saw a peacock
What is the poem about? Is the writer telling you something or is it just for fun?			
Layout and organisation Such as: verses, patterns, rhyme. Look for: repetition of words, phrases and verses.			
Language features Look for: metaphors, similes, powerful verbs, precise adjectives.			
My preference Say which one you like and why			

PHOTOCOPIABLE ■SCHOLASTIC
www.scholastic.co.uk

The Frozen Man and Peacock illustrations © Nova Developments; Cold Morning illustration © Ray and Corrine Burrows/Beehive Illustration.

POETRY
UNIT 2 Narrative poetry

Speak and listen for a range of purposes on paper and on screen

Strand 3 Group discussion and interaction
- Plan and manage a group task over time using different levels of planning.
- Understand different ways to take the lead and support others in groups.
- Understand the process of decision making.

Strand 4 Drama
- Reflect on how working in role helps to explore complex issues.
- Use and recognise the impact of theatrical effects in drama.

Read for a range of purposes on paper and on screen

Strand 6 Word structure and spelling
- Spell words containing unstressed vowels.
- Group and classify words according to their spelling patterns and their meanings.

Strand 7 Understanding and interpreting texts
- Make notes on and use evidence from across a text to explain events or ideas.
- Explore how writers use language for comic and dramatic effects.

Strand 8 Engaging with and responding to texts
- Compare how a common theme is presented in poetry, prose and other media.

Write for a range of purposes on paper and on screen

Strand 9 Creating and shaping texts
- Reflect independently and critically on own writing and edit and improve it.
- Adapt non-narrative forms and styles to write fiction or factual texts, including poems.

Strand 12 Presentation
- Use a range of ICT programs to present texts, making informed choices of which electronic tools to use for different purposes.

Progression in poetry

In this year, children are moving towards:
- Discussing a poet's possible viewpoint, explaining and justifying their own response and interpretation.
- Explaining the use of unusual or surprising language choices and effects, such as onomatopoeia and metaphor; commenting on how this influences meaning.
- Exploring imagery including metaphor and personification.
- Comparing different forms and describing the impact.
- Using carefully observed details and apt images to bring subject matter alive; avoiding cliché in own writing.
- Writing free verse; using or inventing repeating patterns; and attempting different forms, including rhyme for humour.

UNIT 2 ◄ Narrative poetry *continued*

Key aspects of learning covered in this Unit

Enquiry
Children will investigate an older narrative poem, seeking the answers to their own and others' questions. They will engage in drama and discussion and then plan and present their own version orally and visually.

Information processing
Children will identify relevant information from a range of sources and use this as a basis for a choral performance of their own version of the poem.

Evaluation
Children will present information orally, through drama and in writing. They will discuss success criteria, give feedback to others and judge the effectiveness of their own work.

Self-awareness
Children will discuss and reflect on their personal responses to the poems.

Communication
Children will develop their skills to reflect critically on what they have seen and read. They will develop their ability to present a poem orally and reflect critically on their own and others' work.

Prior learning

Before starting this Unit check that the children can:
■ Use drama strategies to aid understanding of texts.
■ Explain how writers use figurative and expressive language to create images and atmosphere.
■ Refer to the text in order to support a hypothesis.
■ Prepare poems for performance.
If they need further support, please refer to a prior Unit or a similar Unit in Year 4.

Resources

The Visitor by Ian Serraillier ❧; *The Bully Asleep* by John Walsh ❧; Photocopiable page 183 'Characters in poems'; Photocopiable page 184 'Poem comparison'; Photocopiable page 185 'Decision-making cards'; Photocopiable page 186 'Evaluation cards'; Assessment activity 'Working in a group 2' ❧

Cross-curricular opportunities

ICT

UNIT 2 ■ Teaching sequence

Phase	Children's objectives	Summary of activities	Learning outcomes
1	I can explore effects of the choice of vocabulary in the text. I can identify poetic techniques used to create tension. I can identify structure of the narrative poem and use role play to explore complex issues.	Read *The Visitor* and explore key vocabulary and phrases to create atmosphere. Children write their own responses to the vocabulary. Identify aspects of *The Visitor* that create tension, such as rhyme. The children explore ways of performing that show the tension. Use *The Visitor* to identify structure. Hot-seat characters in the poem to identify motivations and reasons for behaviour.	Children can express both orally and in writing the effects of language. Children can show through performance how tension is created in the poem. Children can produce an oral outcome using their questioning techniques.
2	I can record opinions or thoughts about events in the poem in a first-person diary account. I can work in role to infer or deduce ideas about character. I can compare how a common theme is presented in different poems.	Read the poem *The Bully Asleep*. Identify similarities and differences between this and *The Visitor*. Choose one of the characters to write their own diary entry about creating back story. Hot-seat each of the different characters in the poem. Generate key questions to ask them. Children write own first-person responses as the different characters from the interview. Create comparison chart. Read *The Bully Asleep*. Identify language features, structure and organisation of this and *The Visitor*.	Children can write a diary entry in the first person about the characters in the poem. Children can record character inferences. Children can compare two poems.
3	I can identify key moments in the narrative. I can plan and manage group tasks over time. I can select parts of the text to present in another form. I can understand different ways to take the lead and support others in the group. I can select parts of the text to present in another form. I can understand different ways to take the lead and support others in the group. I can evaluate my own work according to agreed criteria.	Use either *The Bully Asleep* or *The Visitor*. Plot key moments in the narrative. The children choose one or two key moments to recreate in their own way using phrases from the poem. The children write their own script together for the performance of an extract from the poem. In an ICT suite create a multimedia presentation file, using either downloaded images (copyright permitting) or digital photos of the children's still pictures, adding in sound effects as necessary or aspects of their scripts. The children evaluate together the whole process of writing and performing their own version of the poem, discussing what they would do differently next time. They write their own evaluation of the group work and the outcome).	Children can work collaboratively, deciding on the selection of pictures. Children can identify a collaborative script identified for their own version. Children can create a group ICT file for presentation of their own narrative poem. Children can record own evaluations of work and performance.

Provide copies of the objectives for the children.

DAY 1 ▪ The Visitor

Key features	Stages	Additional opportunities
Enquiry: to explore the effects of the choice of vocabulary in the text	**Introduction** Introduce the children to the Unit by recapping what they know about the structure and language features of poetry. Record their ideas on a board. Discuss with them what poems are usually about. Ensure they understand that writers often write poetry for fun, to tell a story, to comment about something and so on. Draw on their prior knowledge of poems read to give examples. Show the children *The Visitor* by Ian Serraillier from the CD-ROM. Read the poem aloud to them and ask them to identify what type of poem it is. Agree that it is a narrative poem. Read the poem again, this time pausing on key words and phrases, for example *gouged out grave and bone.* Discuss with the children the kinds of images or pictures that come into their heads. Clarify that each individual's images will be different. Encourage the children to talk to each other about the pictures they get in their heads. **Independent work** Provide the children with copies of the text. Get them to identify and explain key images in writing, starting with the lead sentence: *The picture I get in my head is...* Focus on the following words and phrases: *Waves gouged out grave and bone, a ring on a bony hand, Crumbling churchyard, torn from her grasp.* **Plenary** Take feedback from the children. Encourage them to identify powerful verbs as a technique for creating effective images.	**Spelling:** use part of the lesson to revise work on words containing unstressed vowels **Extend:** ensure the children explain the effect of the imagery in their writing **Support:** provide a list of key phrases you want the children to identify and explain

DAY 2 ▪ Creating tension

Key features	Stages	Additional opportunities
Enquiry: to identify techniques the writer uses to create tension	**Introduction** Return to the poem *The Visitor.* Discuss with the children what techniques the writer has used to make it a poem with suspense and atmosphere. Encourage them to think about the setting, language chosen and content. Lead a discussion about what the two main characters have done and the effects of their actions. Explain that the children are going to get to know the poem better by finding ways to perform it. Discuss how they would divide up the poem to show the different voices and what sound effects they could use to create some of the atmosphere.	
Communication: understand the different ways to take the lead and support others in a group	**Independent work and Speaking and listening** Divide the children into groups of four. Encourage them to look through the text for all the clues that tell them how the voices should sound and get them to text mark them so parts are identified. Allow 10–15 minutes for rehearsal and refining of performances. Remind the children that in a group situation they will need to collaborate, discuss and agree together on decisions taken. Invite groups to perform their oral versions. Discuss with the class how they created the tension and what clues they used from the text. **Plenary** Return to the text and identify with the children some of the key phrases that add tension and suspense to the poem, for example short sentences (*He said not a thing*); use of reporting clauses (*a chill voice cried*).	**Extend:** allow opportunities for experimentation in performance **Support:** carefully select the working groups so personalities are supported

DAY 3 ■ How is it put together?

Key features	Stages	Additional opportunities
	Introduction Return to the poem *The Visitor*. Explain to the children that they are going to identify how the poem has been put together – its structure. Provide them with copies of the text and, in pairs, ask them to identify setting, character, problem (link to narrative) and also any aspects of poetry they can see, such as rhyme, repetition, simile, metaphor, organisation of verses and so on. Allow four minutes for the activity. Take feedback from the pairs and, using a copy of the text, record the children's comments and observations. Point out that aspects of the narrative form (story) have been used in a poetic form and this makes it a narrative poem. Ask the children to provide examples of what these aspects might be.	discuss the difference between different types of questions – open, closed, follow-up
Self-awareness: use role play to explore complex issues	**Speaking and listening** Explain to the children that they are going to find out more about the characters by interviewing them, using the hot-seat technique. Using individual whiteboards, ask the children in pairs to record some questions they would like to ask the three characters in the poem. Choose a member of the class to be the skeleton. Carry out the interviews, intervening as necessary, to ensure that the class finds out why the ring was so precious. Continue the interviews, this time finding out what made the man want to pick up the ring in the first place. Did he know he might have done wrong?	**Extend:** encourage the use of open and probing questions **Support:** provide small question prompts
	Plenary Read the poem again to the children and discuss how it is different now that they have explored the characters' motivations for what they are doing. Record the children's comments.	

Guided reading
Read with the children a number of different narrative poems, such as *The Listeners* by Walter de la Mare, *The Pied Piper of Hamlin* by Robert Browning and so on.
Discuss how the narrative structure is used in a poetic form.
Take time also to discuss the effects of different word choices on the reader.

Assessment
Through informal assessment, observation and discussion at whole class and group level, monitor the children's ability to explain the effects of imagery on the reader.
Refer back to the learning outcomes on page 175.

Further work
Encourage the children to have a go at writing their own haunted poem using the structure of *The Visitor* as a starting point. Encourage them to draw on their own experiences of when they have been frightened or experienced something scary at night, for example.

DAY 1 ▪ The Bully Asleep

Key features	Stages	Additional opportunities
Enquiry: to record thoughts or opinions about events or characters in the poem in a first person diary	**Introduction** Read the children the poem, *The Bully Asleep* from the CD-ROM. Identify, through discussion, what is similar between this poem and *The Visitor* – both are narrative poems where poetic devices have been used differently. Briefly identify the poetic structure used in *The Bully Asleep*. Discuss with the class what evidence there is in the poem that shows how these children feel about Billy Craddock. Use paired talk to stimulate discussion. Record some of the children's ideas about the characters'. **Independent work** Provide the children with copies of the text and ask them to choose a character – Jimmy, Jane or Roger. Ask them to start a diary for their character that records what happened in the scene in class that day and how they felt about it. Remind them to read for evidence in the poem of how the characters are feeling towards Billy. Provide them with a starting sentence: *Today in class Billy Craddock fell asleep. Every one was looking at him.* **Plenary** Ask the children to read some of their diary extracts. As they read, return to the text of the poem to check for evidence that has allowed them to draw the inferences they have in their writing.	**Spelling:** use part of the lesson to revise work on words containing unstressed vowels **Extend:** ask the children to find out about more than one child **Support:** direct children to a character and provide simple questions to find out about the character from the text

DAY 2 ▪ What do they think?

Key features	Stages	Additional opportunities
Communication: to work in role to infer and deduce ideas about a characters	**Introduction** Return to *The Bully Asleep*. Explain to the children that they are going to try to capture all the different thoughts and feelings about the characters in the text. Discuss with the children the different characters' responses to each other and the situation. Highlight the references on the text. **Speaking and listening** Use hot-seating to find out more about the characters. Ask the children to discuss the questions they would like to ask. Carry out hot-seating with one child at a time taking on the role of a character and the class asking them questions. Encourage the children to use follow-up questions. As each character has been interviewed, collate their responses in a way that resembles photocopiable page 183 'Characters in poems'. **Independent work** Provide the children with copies of the text and the photocopiable. Use this to record the different perspectives of the characters. Remind them to use the first person for each character. **Plenary** Discuss with the children how working in role helped them to explore the complex issues.	**Extend:** develop the idea of probing questions with the children **Support:** provide a simple frame to record the perspectives of the characters

DAY 3 ■ Compare and contrast narrative poems

Key features	Stages	Additional opportunities
Enquiry: compare how a common theme is presented in different poems	**Introduction** Create a comparison chart that is similar to photocopiable page 184 on a flipchart or whiteboard and provide the children with copies of both *The Visitor* and *The Bully Asleep*. Discuss with them similarities and differences between the two poems, using the following categories: theme, structure and organisation, characters, plot and so on. Model for the children how to explain in writing the images that the writer has used, as well as the other features. Remind them of the need for full sentences in this activity. **Independent work** Provide copies of photocopiable page 184 'Poem comparison' for the children. Working in pairs, ask them to complete the sheet, identifying in as much detail as possible the language features and other features they know about their poems. Remind them that they need to explain their thoughts in as much detail as possible. **Plenary** In whole-class discussion draw the children's attention to the similarities and differences between the poems. Discuss in more detail the themes in each poem. Why do the children think that Ian Serraillier and John Walsh chose to write about these ideas? What do they think they were trying to say?	**Extend:** ensure children provide detailed references to text in their responses **Support:** modify the grid provided to support the lower ability by using simple questions that practice retrieving information

Guided reading
Read with the children a number of different narrative poems, for example *The Listeners* by Walter de la Mare, *The Pied Piper of Hamelin* by Robert Browning and so on.
Discuss how the narrative structure is used in a poetic form.
Take time also to discuss the effects of different word choices on the reader.

Assessment
Through children's responses, oral and written, informally assess the extent to which they are able to infer and deduce characters' behaviour and motivations.
Refer back to the learning outcomes on page 175.

Further work
Encourage the children to have a go at writing a poem using the structure of *The Bully Asleep*.
Use drama techniques to explore the effects of bullying. Link this to the school's anti-bullying policy and PSHE.

DAY 1 ■ Developing own versions

Key features	Stages	Additional opportunities
Self-awareness: plan and manage a group task over time understand the process of decision making	**Introduction** Ensure that everyone has copies of the two poems: *The Visitor* and *The Bully Asleep*. Explain to the children that, over the next three days' lessons, they are going to work to put together their own version of one of the poems. Explain that they are going to create their own script and digital pictures to go with the text. Today's lesson will focus on selecting key parts of the text and creating still pictures to go with them. Divide the children into mixed-ability groups and provide them with decision-making cards, photocopiable page 185. Remind them that their own versions still need to tell the story. Explain that they need to choose four key moments from the story and the phrases that they think best exemplify those moments. **Speaking and listening** In groups, the children select aspects of the text that they want to exemplify. Provide them with the criteria for group organisation (photocopiable page 185). When they have selected the parts of the text they want, they need to organise and create the still pictures for each part. Use a digital camera to record these. **Plenary** Each group shows their still pictures and the lines that go with them to the rest of the class. Has each group identified the main parts of the story?	children could create illustrations to provide a visual cue for their part of the text or use pictures **Extend:** encourage the children to use their own phrases based on the stories told by the poems **Support:** provide a checklist of criteria for children to use for their own version of the poem

DAY 1 ■ Creating a script

Key features	Stages	Additional opportunities
Communication: select parts of the text to use to present in another form **Self-awareness:** understand different ways to take the lead and support others in the group	**Introduction** Recap with the children on the work achieved yesterday. Explain that today they are going to put these elements together to work towards a script and performance. Model how the script might look. Clarify ground rules with them: ■ All children in the group must have a speaking role. ■ Sound effects can be used. ■ The different sections must be joined. ■ The script must be something that all agree on and are clear about what they are saying. ■ The script can use some of the words in the poem but must not be a direct copy. It must show a link between the images created. **Independent work** The children work collaboratively with their pictures (print these out for the groups) to create the script. Ensure they have copies of the text to refer back to. Remind them about selecting appropriate words and phrases. **Plenary** Discuss how effectively the groups worked together. Ask each group to give themselves a score between one and five. Discuss their scores and comments.	**Extend:** children insert their digital pictures into a file during an ICT or literacy lesson and use the file to present their own versions of the poems **Support:** support children to group and classify words according to their spelling patterns

DAY 3 ■ Presenting poem in another form

Key features	Stages	Additional opportunities
Communication: select parts of the text to present in another form	**Introduction** Use this session to make cross-curricular links in ICT. Remind the children of how to insert photos into either a word-processing or multimedia program. Explain that they need to use their scripts to ensure that all members of the group know their cues and where sound effects occur. **Speaking and listening** The children work in groups to refine their presentation, adding phrases and excerpts from the poems to their versions. Explain that they need to be prepared to present their versions of the narrative poems at the end of the lesson, so they will need to rehearse. **Plenary** The children present their own versions of narrative poems. If time allows and facilities are available, video each performance for final evaluation in tomorrow's lesson. After each group's performance, encourage the other children to reflect on the performances by using agreed criteria: ■ Were all members of the group involved? ■ How did the images support the telling of the story of the poem? ■ Were the sound effects used well? ■ How could they have enhanced the performance?	**Extend:** children use ICT skills to present their versions of the poem **Support:** ensure all the children are engaged with the task

DAY 4 ■ How was my presentation?

Key features	Stages	Additional opportunities
Evaluation: evaluate own work according to agreed criteria	**Introduction** As a whole class, briefly recap the three stages of the presentation from Days 1 to 3, selecting key points of the narrative and creating images, writing the script to link each part together, creating the multimedia or word-processed presentation and performing it. Use one group as an example to show children how to discuss how they worked together at each part of the process. Ask the group to give positives and negatives of the experience and then use the interactive assessment 'Working in a group 2' from the CD-ROM. Show the children the performances recorded yesterday and discuss how these went. **Independent work** Ask each group to appoint a scribe to record the group's evaluation. Using photocopiable page 186 'Evaluation cards' to support their discussions, the children write their own evaluation of their group's performance and identify group and personal goals for improvement in group work. **Plenary** As a class, come together to discuss their group work. Ask a member from each group to give an evaluation of their group's work orally. Provide feedback.	**Extend:** children identify personal goals for working in a group and developing their teamwork **Support:** support and structure the discussions by providing clear guidelines for discussion topics

Guided reading

Continue to read with the children a number of different narrative poems, for example *The Listeners* by Walter de la Mare, *The Pied Piper of Hamlin* by Robert Browning and so on.

Discuss how the narrative structure is used in a poetic form.

Take time also to discuss the effects of different word choices on the reader.

Assessment

Informally monitor the children's development in speaking and listening, particularly in group discussion and interaction.

Complete the interactive assessment activity 'Working in a group 2' if not completed previously.

Refer back to the learning outcomes on page 175.

Further work

Develop the children's skill in creating presentations using multimedia or word-processing programs.

Characters in poems

■ Use this chart to record the different perspectives of the characters.

Illustration © Dusan Pavlic / Beehive Illustration

Poem comparison

	The Visitor	The Bully Asleep
Theme *What is the poem mainly about?*		
Structure and organisation *Number of verses, rhymes, repeated lines, use of dialogue*		
Characters *Main characters and secondary characters – what do they do?*		
Story telling *How does the poem tell a story? What is the plot/ problem in the story?*		
Language features *Alliteration, metaphors, powerful verbs, adjectives, imagery such as similes*		

Decision-making cards

✂ --

Decision-making card 1
Group organisation

Choose people in your group to take on the following roles for the task:
- Timekeeper.
- A note-taker to write down all the decisions that your group makes.
- A leader to make sure that every body has a chance to speak.

Rules for the task:
- Make sure you have copies of the poems.
- Highlight carefully the part of the poem you want to use.

✂ --

Decision-making card 2

Decision-making criteria for picking great moments!
- Choose four moments from the poem that you will use for your abridged version of the poem.
- Make sure that the moments you choose are key parts of the story.
- Choose lines from the poem that can give people opportunities to take on roles or act out the moment.
- Make sure the four parts of the poem that you choose tell the story of the poem.

REMEMBER TO RECORD CAREFULLY THE PART OF THE POEM YOU WANT TO USE ON YOUR COPY OF THE POEM

Name _____   Date _____

Evaluation cards

✂

Evaluation card 1

Discuss with your group and give yourselves a score (5 being great – 1 not so great)

Listening	1	2	3	4	5
Turn taking	1	2	3	4	5
Decision making	1	2	3	4	5

Comments _____

Recorded by group scribe   Signature _____

Evaluation card 2

Discuss with your group and give yourselves a score (5 being great – 1 not so great)

Were all the group involved in the presentation?	1	2	3	4	5
Did the pictures/digital photographs support the telling of the story?	1	2	3	4	5
Were the sound effects you used effective and relevant?	1	2	3	4	5

Comments _____

Recorded by group scribe   Signature _____

Summary evaluation card 3
What were the things that went well? _____

_____

_____

What were the aspects that your group needed to work on? _____

_____

_____

POETRY
UNIT 3 Performance poetry

Speak and listen for a range of purposes on paper and on screen

Strand 4 Drama
■ Use and recognise the impact of theatrical effects in drama.

Read for a range of purposes on paper and on screen

Strand 7 Understanding and interpreting texts
■ Infer writers' perspectives from what is written and from what is implied.
■ Explore how writers use language for comic and dramatic effects.
Strand 8 Engaging with and responding to texts
■ Compare the usefulness of techniques, such as visualisation, prediction, empathy in exploring the meaning of texts.
■ Compare how a common theme is presented in poetry, prose and other media.

Write for a range of purposes on paper and on screen

Strand 9 Creating and shaping texts
■ Reflect independently and critically on own writing and edit and improve it.
■ Adapt non-narrative forms and styles to write fiction or factual texts, including poems.
Strand 12 Presentation
■ Use a range of ICT programs to present texts, making informed choices of which electronic tools to use for different purposes.
■ Adapt handwriting for specific purposes, for example printing, use of italics.

Progression in Poetry

In this year, children are moving towards:
■ Varying pitch, pace, volume, expression and using pauses to create impact.
■ Using actions, sound effects, musical patterns, images and dramatic interpretation.

Key aspects of learning covered in this Unit

Enquiry
Children will investigate an older narrative poem, seeking the answers to their own and others' questions. They will engage in drama and discussion and then plan and present their own version orally and visually.

Information processing
Children will identify relevant information from a range of sources and use this as a basis for a choral performance of their own version of the poem.

Evaluation
Children will present information orally, through drama and in writing. They will discuss success criteria, give feedback to others and judge the effectiveness of their own work.

Self-awareness
Children will discuss and reflect on their personal responses to the poems.

Communication
Children will develop their skills to reflect critically on what they have seen and read. They will develop their ability to present a poem orally and reflect critically on their own and others' work.

Prior learning

Before starting this Unit check that the children can:
■ Vary volume, pace and use appropriate expression when performing.
■ Use actions, sound effects, musical patterns and images to enhance a poem's meaning.
■ Identify the characteristics of a performance poem.
If they need further support please refer to a prior Unit or a similar Unit in Year 4.

Resources

Gran Can You Rap? by Jack Ousby ✣; *Fairground* (poem and audio) by Campbell Perry ✣; *Wings* by Pie Corbett ✣; *Whose Dem Boots?* by Valerie Bloom ✣; *Face* (poem and audio) by Campbell Perry ✣; Assessment activity Performance poetry ✣.

Cross-curricular opportunities

Music

UNIT 3 ■ Teaching sequence

Phase	Children's objectives	Summary of activities	Learning outcomes
1	I can identify the key features of poems that make good performance poetry. I can identify the key features of poems that make good performance poetry.	Use both audio and written versions of poems to discuss how poems are made to be performed. Discuss and identify key techniques used in writing and performing. Children select and present poems against identified criteria.	Children can identify the key features of performance poetry. Children can apply varied tone-repeated patterns to range of poems when performing.
2	I can write my own performance poem using identified features. I can use a range of ICT programs to present texts. I can revise and improve writing by developing editing skills. I can use a range of ICT programs to present texts. I can review my own performance against agreed criteria.	Teacher models innovating on one of the poems, such as *Gran Can you Rap?*, writing performance poem using techniques identified. The children work in pairs to write their own performance poems collaboratively and devise ways of performing them. Children perform poems, digitally video them and use an evaluation criteria list to assess their performances	Children can write poems to reflect the identified techniques of performance poetry. Children can collaborate together to create a new performance poem using the best features from the poems they have written. Children can review own learning and evaluate it against clear criteria.

Provide copies of the objectives for the children.

DAY 1 ■ Gran Can You Rap?

Key features	Stages	Additional opportunities
Enquiry: to identify the key features of poems that make good performance poetry	**Introduction** Using the poem *Gran Can You Rap?* from the CD-ROM and identify the key features of performance poetry with the children via shared reading, for example repetitive lines, rhyme, particular rhythm and so on. In particular, focus on the onomatopoeic language *bim, bam, boom* as well as the refrains at the end of each verse. Discuss with the children how the auditory version makes use of these techniques to really perform the poem. Begin to create a list of features of performance poetry on the board. **Independent work** Provide groups of children with different verses of the poem. Encourage them to experiment with the verse and explore different ways of performing it. Share performances at the end of the lesson and begin to draw together the features the poems need to have in order to make them effective poems to perform. **Plenary** Listen to and read the poem *Fairground* from the CD-ROM. Discuss with the children the different structures that the poet uses to make a performance poem.	provide opportunities to read and respond to a variety of performance poems by different writers, such as Michael Rosen, Roger McGough, Wes McGee, Tony Mitton **Extend:** provide success criteria for performances **Support:** provide fewer verses to perform

DAY 2 ■ What makes a performance poem work?

Key features	Stages	Additional opportunities
Evaluation: to identify the key features of poems that make good performance poetry	**Introduction** Recap with the children the features of performance poems discussed on Day 1. Provide them with copies of *Who Dem Boots*, *Face* and *Wings* from the CD-ROM. Remind them of the criteria identified for the features of performance poetry. In groups, the children read the poems and identify whether the features are present. Focus their attention not only on structural devices for performance but the choice of words, how they are combined, use of detail, powerful verbs and adjectives. Take feedback from the children and record any further criteria they have noticed on the board. **Independent work** In pairs, the children devise ways of performing the poems. Remind them to focus on ways of creating effective use of the features, for example changing volume, pace, expression and movement, as well as adding simple music or percussion. **Plenary** Return the children's attention to the checklist of features of performance poetry and allow groups to evaluate their performances.	**Extend:** identify all features of performance poetry, especially the effect of powerful verbs, rhythms and adjectives **Support:** use four main features in their performances, such as action, tone of voice, percussive sound

Guided reading
Use guided reading time to support children's ability to infer and deduce a writer's opinion from what is implied in the text.

Assessment
Use observation of performances to informally assess children's speaking and listening skills. Discuss how use of tone, action and sound can affect a performance. Refer back to the learning outcomes on page 189.

Further work
Read a variety of poems out loud at story time or visit poetry websites to hear/see poems in performance. Discuss their preferences with the children.

DAY 1 ■ Writing my own performance poem

Key features	Stages	Additional opportunities
Information processing: write own performance poem using identified features	**Introduction** Return the children to the list of features of performance poems created in Phase 1, Days 1 and 2 of this Unit. Explain to the children that they are going to write their own performance poetry, using and applying some of the key features identified through reading. Remind them of the different poems that they have read, discussing the content, for example. *Gran Can You Rap?*, *Fairground, Whose Dem Boots*, and *Face*. Identify the different subject matter in the poems and how the authors patterned them. Use paired talk to identify potential subject matter for their own poems. Remind the children that they could innovate on the poems read to help them with the writing process. As a starting point, suggest that they use the technique of alteration to begin their writing, for example *Dad can rap*, or *Wear dem Shoes*, or *A grin says OK.* **Independent work** The children decide on the subject matter for their different performance poems and write them, using some of the ideas and models shown in the modelled writing session. Remind them of the list of different features that they identified in previous lessons to include in their performance poems. **Plenary** The children provide feedback on their poems and discuss the strategies and techniques that they have used to make them performance poems.	use the time to revise work on alliteration, rhythm and rhyme in poetry **Extend:** allow the children to choose the subject matter and structure for their poems **Support:** provide one verse of *Gran Can You Rap?* with deleted words and lines for children to innovate on

DAY 2 ■ Writing performance poems collaboratively

Key features	Stages	Additional opportunities
Evaluation: revise and improve writing by developing editing skills	**Introduction** Explain to the children that they are going to work together to revise and edit their poems and, through the process, create new poems by taking the best lines, phrases and patterns from their old ones. Using an example of the children's work from Day 1 of this Phase, discuss with them the lines, phrases and techniques that have been used that they consider are effective. Model how to put these into a new poem on an agreed subject matter. Itemise the stages the children need to go through: ■ Read both poems and identify the best phrases, lines and words. ■ Agree a new subject matter or the same subject matter. ■ Draft together a new performance poem, adding together new ideas and the best lines of the poems. **Independent work** Put the children in pairs. Provide them with copies of their poems and a collaborative sheet so that they can develop and extend their ideas for their new poems. **Plenary** The children provide feedback to the class on the changes made to their poems and the techniques they have used.	**ICT:** use a word processing package to redraft the poems and use different fonts, sizes, styles and layouts **Extend:** record/ write their own poems individually **Support:** provide a structure for their poems, such as number of lines, patterning

DAY 3 ■ Performing our poems

Key features	Stages	Additional opportunities

Stages

Introduction
Explain the focus of the lesson to the children: to find ways to perform their redrafted collaborative poems. Recap strategies for performance with them: use of volume and tone, expression and movement, pace, addition of music, rhythm and body percussion.

Speaking and listening
Provide the children with a short time frame in which to prepare their poems for performance. Remind them of important strategies for working together, for example listening, negotiating and so on. Allow time for them to revise their performances, focusing on the different aspects.

Plenary
Allow time for each pair to perform their poems. Ask the listeners to provide oral feedback on the performances along the criteria outlined, for example pace, variance of volume and tone and strategies used in the writing.
Use a digital video to record the children's performances. Play the clips back and evaluate their performances. Using whiteboards, ask pairs to record two key points about their performance that they would change as a result of their observations of the video and the feedback from the other children.

Key features
Evaluation: review own performance against agreed criteria

Additional opportunities
Extend: make sure children give detailed evaluation of performances using appropriate vocabulary

Support: use actions, variety of tone and percussion to perform

Guided reading
Use a variety of texts to focus the children's ability to discuss imagery and use of vocabulary to create effects in reading.
Develop the children's ability to discuss and express these thoughts with the use of pictures.

Assessment
Assess the children's performances and poetry by using the key criteria:
■ vary pitch, pace, volume, expression and use pauses to create impact;
■ use actions, sound effects, musical patterns, images and dramatic interpretation.
Use the interactive assessment activity 'Performance poetry' from the CD-ROM.
Refer back to the learning outcomes on page 189.

Further work
Promote a selection of writers of poetry in the book corner in the classroom to develop children's knowledge of writers. Collect recordings of the children's performances to create an audio file using ICT as well as a published anthology.